SINGLE
AND
HAPPY

SINGLE AND HAPPY

Five Practical Steps to
Wholeness in Spirit, Soul and Body
ARE YOU A W.H.O.L.E SINGLE?

GLORIA GODSON

XULON PRESS

Xulon Press
2301 Lucien Way #415
Maitland, Fl 32751
407.339.4217
www.xulonpress.com

Printed in the United States of America.

ISBN-13: 978-1-5456-7148-1

Dedicated

to

Emmanuel, Timothy, and Rhema

and

my friend and partner, Holy Spirit

TABLE OF CONTENTS

INTRODUCTION

MANY ROADS LEAD TO ADULT SINGLENESS. For some, the road traveled was paved with the heartache of loss through death, others traveled the heart wrenching path of marital breakup and divorce, and yet for some others, they have not yet met that special someone, and so, have traveled the lonely road of prolonged singleness. In each instance, the path traveled is different, but the journey, and the associated challenges are not unique. They are common to all. Whatever your path to singleness, whether it is a straight path of prolonged waiting for that right person, or your road took a sharp U turn and brought you right back to a state of singleness after years of marriage, God has a plan for your life, all of it, including the single seasons. Your current singleness did not take God by surprise. He has a plan for it and for you. He is the God who changes times and seasons (Daniel 2:21). He wants to be Lord of every season of your life, and He wants you to be whole, purposeful, and fruitful in every season.

What is your road to singleness? Understanding and making peace with your current single status is very important to wholeness. Being able to tell your story with self-acceptance, and without bitterness and rancor is a tell-tale sign of your degree or stage of healing, wholeness, and the restorative work of the Holy Spirit in your life. Whether you are single or single again, and whatever the road to your present singleness, God wants you to be WHOLE, and to live a life full of His presence, purpose, passion, and power. This book shows you how.

My Road to Singleness

I gave my life to Christ as a teenager. I fell passionately in love with Jesus Christ, and committed myself to live a life that honors Him. When I went to college, I sought God with my whole heart. He was my primary pursuit. In college, I met a fine young man! He was a leader in the campus Christian fellowship, and well respected. He loved God, and taught the word of God faithfully. We fell in love and got married. As far as I was concerned, that marriage was for life! I strongly disapproved of divorce, did not believe in it, and spoke out vociferously against it. My motto was, God hates divorce, and so do I!

We were married for over 18 years. We had many happy years. However, in the last few years of our marriage, my ex-husband was attacked by the enemy. Wrong mindsets, pride, a love of money, and a get-rich-quick mentality eventually led to major breaches in character and fidelity. Unbeknownst to me, he got involved in questionable business transactions, and when they went south, he skipped town.

Overnight, I was thrust into singleness, and single parenthood of three children. More than that, his actions ruined other people, and devastated many who had trusted him. I was deeply grieved, beyond my ability to express in words! How could a good man, with so much potential, make such a colossal shipwreck? How could he intentionally hurt and abandon his family? How could he run like a coward, and leave his family, including his baby girl, to face the consequences of his actions? This was not the man I married, what happened?

I was severely disappointed in myself. How did I get into this ditch? I wanted to know what happened. I had many questions. Did I make a mistake? Did I marry the wrong man? Did I not hear from God in marrying him? How could a good man go so bad? How do I fix this? How can I help rebuild the lives he destroyed? How do I pick up the pieces? How do I and my kids move forward? How will this affect my teenage sons? What about my baby girl? She was such a daddy's girl; how would she make it without him? What are my next steps?

I was disappointed in God. I knew God did not do this to me, but how could He let this happen to me? I have loved, honored, and served the Lord faithfully since teen age. In obedience to the Word of God, I had forgiven and overlooked egregious issues, and worked determinedly to build my home. In the last several months, my efforts to restore and strengthen our marriage included holding him accountable for various actions, and requiring change in behavior, and not just verbal affirmations, and empty promises. I knew that he did not like that, but I also knew that this was the only way that we could move forward and heal. What I did not realize was how much he resented me for it. I could not believe that he would deliberately plan and execute this level of treachery against me, and his own kids. The multitude of lies and deception was staggering. I felt betrayed, exploited, and used, and in my heart, I blamed God for it. It was obedience to His word that got me in this situation.

I struggled with trust. I was suspicious of everyone, especially men. I did not want anything to do with them. I was hurting so bad. I took my broken heart and life to the Lord. My identity as a daughter of God was severely challenged. I am usually a very confident woman, but I suffered self-doubt, and questioned God's love for me, and His faithfulness to His word. I was thrust into a place that I never imagined that I would ever be, and I wondered, "Where is my God?"

During this time, it was very hard to come to church. My innate urge was to run away, or to go to another church, where I was anonymous, and can grieve, and mourn in private. But I refused to run, and chose rather to stand in the glare of public scrutiny. Sunday after Sunday, I grit my teeth and came to church. Often, I was met at the door by folks who were involved in the fiasco with my ex-husband, who had a question or an

issue to discuss. The devil and my flesh wanted me to
hide, and stay away from church, and Christian fellowship, but the Holy Spirit instructed me to come, and
enabled me to do so week after week. His emphasis was
clear. I needed to be in fellowship with other Christians.
I needed to stay connected to the body of Christ, regardless of how uncomfortable it was. I felt a little like Jesus
who was publicly crucified for the sins of others, but did
not open His mouth. It was a very humbling time, and
I spent a lot of it on my knees. Prayer was my lifeline.
I desperately clung to God in prayer. Over the years, I
had established personal altars, a scheduled time in the
day, week, and month that I set aside to seek God privately in prayer, and sometimes fasting. These personal
altars saved me! Though I questioned the love of God,
the unfairness of what happened to me, and the faithfulness of God, these personal altars drove me to God.

> *Over the years, I had established personal
> altars, a scheduled time in the day, week, and
> month that I set aside to seek God privately
> in prayer, and sometimes fasting. These
> personal altars saved me!*

I ran to God, because I was used to spending those
times with Him, and had nowhere else to go. I had a
prior longstanding commitment to meet with God in

prayer at certain times, and I kept my prayer appointments with God. Most of the time, I didn't have any
words, so I simply brought my tears. I felt resentful
and abandoned by God, but I came anyway, to my
meeting with God. I didn't have faith filled words or
even nice thoughts about God. I felt betrayed and let
down, but I came anyway. Sometimes, my thoughts
about God were downright angry and disrespectful, but
I came anyway. I didn't say much to Him and didn't
want to, but I came anyway. I didn't know how to pray
or what to pray for, so I prayed mostly in the spirit.
Those daily, weekly, and monthly times alone with God
literally saved my life. I have always had a fearless faith,
and bold confidence in the unwavering love of God for
me. Now, that unquestioning trust was broken, and I
was afraid. I wondered, "If God allowed this travesty to
happen to me, what else might He allow? Can I really
trust Him to protect me?" I felt trapped and hopeless,
and thought of suicide. Again, and again I buckled to
my knees in sheer desperation. I needed God desperately. I was angry, upset, and disappointed with God,
but I needed Him to make it through each day. From
the practical challenges of running back and forth to
take my teenage boys to and from football practice;
my daughter to and from daycare; my full time job as
a corporate executive; being a prayer minister, overseer, and Board member at our church; to resolving
the mess left behind by my ex-husband; I needed and
leaned heavily on God. My day typically began well

before dawn each day, and didn't end until close to midnight. I was physically exhausted and emotionally drained most of the time. My hair fell out and I had ringing in my ears. I do not know how I survived that year. The only explanation is the grace and mercy of God. I needed Him every single minute of every day.

My personal "routine" habit of prayer helped me to maintain my sanity and personal equilibrium against incredible odds. I found that God was big enough to handle all my accusations, doubts, questions, fears, unbelief, anger, and resentment. He knew how much I was hurting, and gazed into my tear, and fear filled eyes with intense grace, and unflinching love. Every time I came to meet with Him, He was always there. He kept our appointments, and reassured me with His presence that I was not in this by myself. He never once rebuked me for my doubts and irreverent thoughts. He never pulled back or spoke harshly to me. He simply stayed and loved me through it all. He drenched my soul with refreshing. As I lay prostrate before Him, His loving presence would saturate my scorched soul and wash over me like gentle waves over a parched, and barren desert. Sometimes, I was so physically and emotionally depleted, drained, and bone-weary that I would just drift off to sleep in His presence and wake up rejuvenated, revived, and strengthened to go another day, or week, or month.

> *I found that God was big enough to handle
> all my accusations, doubts, questions, fears,
> unbelief, anger, and resentment.*

At church, I continued to lead corporate prayer. I talked to God and poured out my heart before Him. Unfortunately, there are some people at church who like to talk about things they do not know. So, they talked, and worst of all, instead of having the courage to come up to me to ask their questions, they cornered my children at church, and barraged them with questions to satisfy their curiosity. My kids felt wounded, exposed, and bludgeoned. I felt vulnerable and besieged.

But, I could not afford the luxury of "falling apart". Too many people were depending on me. I had three children to raise, two teenagers and a toddler, plus, I was a prayer minister, and a corporate executive. I did not tell anyone at work about my troubles. I did not want to drag the problems I was facing at home, and church into my office space. Work provided a refuge for me. My office was a sanctuary. It was the one place where I could be normal, and apply myself productively to achieve business objectives without the distraction of the dysfunction that I was dealing with at home and at church.

It has been several years since. God has healed and restored me. He did not answer all my questions, but He answered some, and asked me to trust Him for the rest. Some questions, He answered with a question of His own. For example, when I repeatedly asked God if I made a mistake in marrying this man, He asked me whether He, God, made a mistake when He chose Saul to be king over Israel. The Lord showed me that His original plan was to establish Saul's kingdom over Israel forever (1 Samuel 13:13-14). But Saul chose the path of disobedience, just like my ex-husband did, and made a ship wreck. God made the right choice, but Saul exercised his free will to made the wrong choice, and took himself right out of God's plan and purpose for his life.

As the Lord began the work of healing and restoration in my heart, I took the initiative to reach out to my ex-husband to let him know that I forgave him, even though he had not apologized or asked for forgiveness. To God's glory, he eventually did ask for forgiveness, and I told him that I had completely forgiven and released him. However, I decided not to get back together with him when he asked me, because I did not see evidence of genuine repentance on his part, and I was not prepared for a rerun of the horrible nightmare I had just been through. Today, I and my children have not only survived, we have thrived! God not only healed me, He made me whole. Today, I am a kept woman, a whole woman, kept by the grace, and power of Almighty God. This book chronicles my journey of survival, the healing process, becoming a W.H.O.L.E Single, and the lessons I learned along the way.

CHAPTER 1
WHOLENESS

SEVERAL YEARS AGO, I WAS ON A PANEL AT a women's conference, and received an anonymous question – "How can I be single and happy?" That question has haunted me since that day, because I was disappointed with myself in the way that I answered it. I gave a flippant response. I basically told the precious woman who asked that question to, "get a life". But I walked away feeling that I had been unfair to her, and keenly aware that I did not know the answer to that question myself. So, over the years, I have pondered, inquired, studied, and researched that question. This book provides the answer. You can be single and happy if you are whole. For a single person, HAPPY is spelt WHOLE.

You can be single and happy if you are whole.
For a single person, HAPPY is spelt WHOLE.

Merriam Webster's dictionary defines "whole" as, "A thing that is complete in itself; all of something; entire;

in an unbroken or undamaged state, in one piece, intact, entire, full, uncut, sum total, unity."

A whole single is a person who is complete in themselves and who they are in Christ, a person who is sufficient, entire, undivided, full, and in one piece. A whole single is a person of strength, dignity, unity, and grace. Whole singles are men and women of tremendous worth who value themselves, own their personal value, and are confident in themselves, and their God. Whole singles are free people who live interesting lives; lives that are free from self-pity, regret, desperation, depression, and low self-esteem. Whole singles are men and women who make a choice daily to honor God in their singleness, invest in the lives of others, and live an abundant life. They are single men and women who act on purpose and with intentionality to impact their world, and transform the lives of people in their sphere of influence - their children, relatives, future spouse, co-workers, friends, and so on. Whole singles are men and women who are comfortable in their own skin, and live lives of purpose, passion, and power.

Whole singles are men and women of tremendous worth who value themselves, own their personal value, and are confident in themselves, and their God.

Simply stated, a whole single is a person who does not have to look outside of themselves and Christ who lives in them, for their sense of self-worth, personal validation, confidence, affirmation, and wellbeing. They know that in Christ, they are enough! They are self-sufficient in Christ's sufficiency. Apostle Paul was a whole single! In Philippians 4:13 (AMP) he said, "I can do all things, which He has called me to do, through Him who strengthens and empowers me to fulfill His purpose. I am self-sufficient in Christ's sufficiency; I am ready for anything and equal to anything through Him who infuses me with inner strength and confident peace." What he is saying is that he finds his confidence, faith, strength, empowerment, purpose, peace, and wellbeing in Christ. He was whole!

W.H.O.L.E

Wholeness is not a reference to physical, mental, or emotional ability, or disability. W.H.O.L.E stands for:

W – WELL
H – HEALTHY
O – ON-FIRE
L – LOVING
E – EMPOWERED

After a decade of successfully living as a single Christian woman, I am convinced beyond any doubt that a single person cannot be whole if they are not well, healthy, on-fire, loving, and empowered. The remaining chapters in this book will discuss these critical steps to wholeness.

Why is Wholeness so Important?

In God's relationship economy, 1 + 1 =1. No other combination gets to the same result. Summing up the account of God's creation of the man and woman in Genesis 2:24-25, the Bible states, "A man shall leave his father and mother and be joined to his wife, and they shall become one." This is God's game plan, his blueprint for marriage. Ephesians 5:31 confirms and emphasizes this point. Put simply, God's relationship plan is, one whole man, plus one whole woman, become one whole bonded unit. This is the divine design. When two whole people are fused into this new entity, they become an explosive, unstoppable force, in the same way that Jesus is with the church (Ephesians 5:22-32). The new undivided unit is powerful beyond the sum of their individual parts. This is God's original idea and this unit is the building block of the family, society, community, nation, and the world.

This is why it poses a major problem when a person who is not whole or complete in themselves, is trying to connect and build a relationship with another person. This is a frustrating and painful enterprise because in God's relationship economy, ¼, ½, or 2/3 + 1 will never equal 1.

In God's relationship economy, 1 + 1 = 1.
No other combination gets to the same result.

In math, whole numbers are numbers that represent unity without pieces. Whole numbers are positive numbers. They are exact numbers. There is no fraction or fragmentation. Whole numbers are unbroken numbers. They are integers. They are precise. This is why wholeness is important. A whole person is a positive person, a person who does not fall to pieces at the whiff of every wind of adversity, a whole person is a person who is clear about who they are, and can articulate with some precision what they want in life, from a relationship, and so on. A whole person is not fragmented, internally disjointed, and conflicted. They are consistent and when you deal with them, you don't have to worry about which person will show up today, because the same person will show up every time. Even before you get to know them well, you get the sense that they have depth and their personal foundation is sound, solid, and safe to build upon. They have the bandwidth and emotional range necessary to sustain a healthy relationship.

Whole people are dependable, steadfast, and reliable. They have integrity and character. They are comfortable in their own skin, and take responsibility, and personal accountability for their lives, choices, and decisions. You don't have to do tricks or jump through hoops to keep a whole person happy. You don't have to exhaust yourself to fill them up by constantly pouring praise, affirmation, and recognition on them. They draw their confidence, self-definition, strength, and identity from their relationship with Christ. That supply never runs out, so they are refilled as needed, and have enough overflow to help others. A whole person always brings something of value to the table, themselves, and they always add value to any environment in which they engage. When you've been with a whole person, you walk away feeling that you have gained from that interaction. This is why wholeness is so important. Wholeness gives life!

> *A whole person always brings something of value to the table, themselves.*

The path to wholeness is a process that restores the broken pieces of a person, resolves fragmentation in the mind, personality, values, thoughts, and beliefs, and provides integrity, consistency, and stability. Simply stated, wholeness allows you to know yourself, and confirm who you are, your values, what is important to you, your self-definition, what you want in a relationship, and so on. This process of self-discovery, self-knowledge, and acceptance is critical to personal well-being, and is indispensable in relationship formation. God's best plan is for this work of redemption and restoration to happen before marriage, but if we are impatient, and hurry into a relationship before the wholeness process completes, this necessary work will then have to be completed within marriage, and this causes significant trauma, and could lead to a cycle of divorces.

Un-Whole Connections

Un-whole Connections are painful. They are connections or relationships between two people who are not whole or between a person who is whole, and another person who is not. Un-whole connections are fraught with difficulties, and here is why:

a. Trying to connect to a person who is not whole is a prickly and abrasive process because pieces of them are missing, dislocated or twisted up into a tangled mess. This could be emotionally, physically, mentally, socially, or relationally. They are not able to meaningfully engage and connect in the area that is lacking. Simply stated, things don't match up. It's like the lights are on, but nobody is home in the area of dysfunction. This can sometimes lead to the heartbreaking situation where you think you know a person, and have been in a relationship with them for a while, then one day, a whole new side of them shows up, and you wonder, "Who is this person?"

b. Jesus tells us to love others as we love ourselves (Mark 12:30-31). Real love is built on a foundation of trust, understanding, and respect. How can you trust, understand, and respect yourself, when you don't even know yourself? Self-love that is not tempered by self-knowledge and awareness, is arrogant and narcissistic. And how can you love another person if you don't love yourself? When a person does not respect or love themselves, they have an insatiable appetite for love and respect that nobody else can fill. It doesn't matter how much their spouse or significant other pours into them, their self-definition is faulty, and because that core foundation is vandalized, the entire cargo of respect leaks out momentarily. It is an exhausting cycle of constantly trying to fill them up, make them feel worthy, respected, loved, and happy, and one single action, word or event undoes all that work, and you have to start all over again, because the leaky valve is inside them, and the solution must come from within. This type of laborious relationship eventually wears the other person out, and leads to a break-up or divorce.

c. One of the decisions every person must make is who they are all by themselves. But, the person who is not whole, looks to others, their spouse, friends, and family to tell them who they are, and to make them feel loved, accepted, and valued. This places a huge unrealistic and undue expectation on the other person to be to them what only God can be. In time, they become demanding, whining, clingy, and a royal pain to be around. Their focus is entirely on themselves, as they are looking to earn, cajole, manipulate, or extort the approval, love, acceptance, and sense of value they so desperately need from the other person. Anything they do "for the other person" is really part of the whole scheme to earn or get them the compliments, comments, recognition, and affirmation they need. Eventually, this self-centeredness will pull the thread, and destroy the fabric of the relationship.

d. The person who is not whole will misinterpret and misunderstand words, gestures, and overtures. They have misplaced internal filters that color interpersonal interactions and everything that they see, hear or experience. They often read the wrong meaning into what is said and will interpret things in the worst possible light. Sometimes, they transpose the pain, distrust or trauma from a prior relationship into their current relationship, and exact from their current relationship, "payment" for past wrong, abuse or breakup. Sometimes they bring with them personal vows that they made to themselves like, - "Nobody will ever do that to me again." Sadly, because of these vows, they are quick to misdiagnose situations, and misinterpret words and actions. Relationships with an un-whole person tends to be stormy, on again and off again, like a roller coaster ride, and often, they quit prematurely on a wrong assumption that most often is not true.

e. A person who is not whole, looks to another person to complete them, whether it is a child, spouse, friend, or other relative. They draw their sense of self-worth from being connected to or needed by this other person. This leads to a co-dependent relationship. Such is the cautionary tale of the single person who gets married so that the other person can make them happy. This only leads to disappointment, bitterness, and disillusionment when inevitably, that person fails, as every human being does. Only Christ and a right relationship with him can fill the aching void in each of us, and our longing for meaning and significance.

Becoming Whole

Becoming whole is a process. It is a healing and restoration project undertaken, and superintended by the Holy Spirit. It is a multi-layered process that exposes and addresses multidimensional issues. Below is an outline of the process:

1. Forgiveness: The first step in the process of becoming whole is to forgive, let go, and release the person who hurt you. For me, this was not easy, but I knew that in order to heal, I needed to forgive. Here are the steps I took:

    a. **First, I Made a Decision to Forgive:** I did not feel like forgiving my ex-husband, nor did I want to forgive him. In fact, I caught myself on several occasions fantasizing about some terrible things happening to him, as he "reaps what he sowed" for all the pain he caused me, my children, and so many people. Then one day, the Lord said to me, "It could be worse, it could have been you. What if it was you who did the things he did?" This question startled me. My initial reaction was, "Of course not, I would never do that!" But as I pondered the question, my attitude began to change. First, it led me to say to myself, "There but for the grace of God go I". This man was a strong Christian leader who impacted the lives of so many, but now has allowed himself to be seduced and led astray by the devil.

James 1:15 describes this seduction process: "Temptation comes from our own desires, which entice us and drag us away. These desires give birth to sinful actions. And when sin is allowed to grow, it gives birth to death." This could happen to anybody. It could very well have been me. That thought caused me to shudder, but it was true. We both grew up in the same campus Christian fellowship, he was an older, and more mature Christian than I was. But here he was, seduced, and taken captive by the deceitfulness of sin (Hebrews 3:13).

Secondly, pondering that question filled me with compassion for him. What a terrible burden to carry, to know that your selfish choices destroyed so many lives? I do not want to have that on my conscience. That burden would be too heavy for me to bear.

Lastly, it helped me to see him through God's eyes. Instead of anger and revenge, I felt sorry for him. What a wreck! A life so full of promise and potential, now in tatters, like the aftermath of a hurricane. It's like the scripture says, "He that sows the wind, shall reap the whirlwind" (Hosea 8:7). After pondering all this, I pulled myself up by my emotional bootstraps and made a decision to forgive him.

b. **Then I Began to Say Those Words Out of My Mouth:** I called his name out aloud and said, "I forgive you". It was very distasteful and heart wrenching. I did not want to say those words. Even though I had decided to forgive, I still did not feel like forgiving. I felt it was unfair and every time I said those words, I wept sorely. The evil that had been perpetrated against me and my children was real, and grossly unfair. I felt like I was condoning or excusing his actions. I felt cheated, used, and abused. But I disciplined myself to say those words, again, and again. I did not believe them or feel them at first. I just said them as a personal commitment out of my mouth.

c. **Next, I Went to God for Help:** I went to God in prayer, told Him I have decided to forgive and asked him to help me. I simply couldn't do it on my own. God asked me to surrender to Him, my right to hurt my ex-husband back. You see, when you are hurt, you earn a right to hurt back the person who hurt you. This right is enshrined under the old covenant. Exodus 21:24-25 states, "an eye for an eye, a tooth for a tooth, a hand for a hand, a foot for a foot, a burn for a burn, a wound for a wound, a bruise for a bruise."

> *We are most like God,*
> *when we forgive those who hurt us.*

You have a choice. You can hold onto this "hurt right" and exercise it yourself, or you can turn it over to God, and set the offender free. That is the essence of forgiveness. Turning your right over to God and leaving it up to Him to deal with it, and the offender as He chooses. Under the new covenant, this is the only option (Matthew 6:15; Romans 12:19). When you release the offender to God, you walk away free. Someone has said that when you forgive, the prisoner you set free is yourself. How true! Giving your "hurt right" to God does not mean that you forget or excuse what happened, or that you "reconcile", and get right back into the same bad situation, but it does mean that you will not hold, use or exercise that right against that person any more. That right now belongs to the Lord.

d. **I Chose to Give My "Hurt Right" to The Lord and That Choice Freed Me:**Forgiveness became a gift I gave to myself. It set me free to heal. I believe that we are most like God, when we forgive those who hurt us. Jesus said that when we love, bless, and pray for those who hurt us, we are, sons of our Father in heaven, "For He makes His sun rise on the evil and on the good, and sends rain on the just and on the unjust" (Matthew 5:44).

Since that time, I have thought about this some more, and have come to the conclusion that forgiveness and giving my "hurt right" to the Lord was the best way to make sure the devil does not win. The whole plan of the devil was to destroy my ex-husband's life, my life, and the lives of our children. My children and I forgiving him ensures that our lives would not be destroyed, and relinquishing our "hurt right" to God, will ensure that, if at all possible, his life will not be destroyed as well. God will work it out in such a way that the devil loses all around.

God owning, and exercising my "hurt right" is the only scenario that has the potential for a redemptive outcome for everyone involved. You see my real enemy is the devil, not my ex-husband. He too, was deceived by the devil. If I take my eyes off him for a minute, and focus on the devil, who perpetrated all this evil, then forgiveness is the only path forward that spoils the devil and the kingdom of darkness. It denies the devil of the trophy of ruined lives that he worked so hard to get.

e. **Then I Began to Pray, Really Pray, for Him:**
I prayed that I forgave him and released him.
I prayed for genuine repentance in his life. I
prayed that it will be well with him and that
God will bless him. I declared that the devil
will not win in his life, but that God will win. I
prayed Ephesians 1:16-21; and 3:14-21 over
him. When I started praying these prayers for
him, I really did not want all these good things
to happen for him. I prayed it as a Christian act
or duty, but as I prayed for him, God blessed
me, my children, and him. God answered my
prayer! Little by little, the pain, and animosity
in my heart decreased. It was like God peeled
it away, one layer at a time, like an onion.
The things that I felt he stole from me, God
restored manifold. God blessed me and my children so much that I didn't mind or begrudge
God blessing him too. Over time, I genuinely
wished him well, wanted good things to happen
to and for him, and was genuinely happy for
him when it did.

2. My Identity in Christ: My next step to wholeness was to take back control of my identity in Christ.
Divorce shook me to my foundation because it violated
one of my core beliefs and caused me to question, and
revisit issues that I thought were settled in my life.
During this dark time, the enemy launched a massive,

multi-step, offensive against my identity, authority, security, and sense of belonging as a daughter of God. In my book, *Choosing a Life of Victory,* I describe in detail the devil's multi step identity theft strategy. Here are some of the steps he used against me:

a. First, he played on my human need to understand and make sense of what happened. He kept an endless barrage of questions flooding my mind. His ultimate bottom line was, "You have been a faithful Christian. Why did you go through this and where is God when you need Him?"

b. Then, he challenged and questioned my trust in God. How can you trust God? If He stood by and allowed these traumatic circumstances to invade your life, how can you trust him to protect you?

c. Next, he challenged and tried to silence my witness, and testimony. "Look at your life", he snickered, "It is a mess. How dare you speak to another person about God? What do you have to say? Your life is a reproach, who will listen to you anyway?"

d. Then he sneered, "God doesn't love you. If He did, why are you going through this? God can deliver you, why doesn't He? Think about it, if it were your son or daughter, would you let him or her go through this if you can stop it? God doesn't care. He delights in seeing you suffer and wants to grind you into the dust". *(Choosing A Life of Victory, Gloria Godson, Xulon Press, 2019).*

This was a devastating cycle of attacks as the devil bombarded my mind with these fiery darts. His goal was to steal my identity in Christ, and in so doing, my access to God's resources. He wanted to render me ineffective, and impotent as a Christian, and ultimately, to drive me to hopelessness, and despair. But the devil is a liar! The Holy Spirit showed me that God has provided a pathway to victory over the devil's identity theft strategy. The pathway is through the word of God. So, I fought back with the word. In my book, *Choosing a Life of Victory*, I explain how:

"Romans 8:31-39 outlines our response to the devil's attacks and gives us a pathway to victory. It tells us to talk back to the devil and gives us what to say. Even if you are still struggling to believe the word of God, do not understand what is going on and cannot see or explain God's workings in your life, you can trust His heart and talk back to the devil with confidence:

   a. God is for me. Tell the devil over and over again, God is for me. I don't know why I am going through this, but one thing I know, God is for me. He is not against me. I am not in this by myself. God is for me (Romans 8:31).

b. God chose me in Christ to be His child. Devil, how dare you accuse me? God justified me and gave me right standing with Himself. I reject every voice of accusation, and judgement (Romans 8:33).

c. Regardless, I will wait on the Lord. I will stay upon His word. I will serve and I will worship. I believe the word of God that this situation is working for me. So, I fix my eyes, not on what I see, but on what is unseen, because what I see is temporal, meaning that it is subject to change, but what is unseen is eternal (2 Corinthians 4:18). Even if this situation on earth does not change, my eternal future is secure in Christ. I know the end of my story, and I win!"

Affirming who I was in Christ and assuring my heart that God, my Father, loved me unconditionally, accepted me, chose me, justified me, and that my divorce did not change any of that, was supremely redemptive, and restorative. God sees me in Christ and He is pleased with me, no matter what. In Christ, I am whole, complete, and secure.

3. Receive God's Love: The next step to wholeness is to accept the unconditional love of God. Divorce was very traumatic for me, because it was a word I never ever considered would be spoken from my lips or in connection with me. But here I was, my ex-husband had absconded, years have passed and I was left to pick up the pieces. When I finally came to terms with the fact that to get my affairs in order legally, I needed to file the divorce papers, I simply couldn't bring myself to do it. Even though I had every ground for divorce provided in the scriptures (Matthew 5:32, 1 Corinthians 7:15), that didn't make it any easier. Eventually, I filled out the papers, but I simply could not bring myself to go and file it. I carried the completed package around in my car for almost a year, while I explored whether I had any other options.

When I finally filed the papers, the devil, and my conscience attacked me viciously. They screamed at me, "Divorcee! Failure! You failed in your marriage! You have done what God hates!" But immediately God stepped up and spoke up for me. His voice was like the sound of many waters, and it drowned out the voice of my accusers. God was speaking hot and holy words of tender, passionate love, and unconditional acceptance. The Lord was jealous over me, and He told me so! He said, "You belong to me!"; "You are precious in my sight!"; "I rejoice over you"; "I am your husband"; "You are dearly beloved!"; and "You are loved with an everlasting love!" The Lord covered me. During that time, I wept continuously. My heart was broken into tiny fragments. He picked them up one by one, and tenderly applied His healing balm to each piece.

You see, I had grown up in a legalistic denomination where you kept your tithe booklet up to date if you wanted to be, "a member in good standing" and you had to live a visibly "holy" life (no makeup, long dresses, hair covering, and so on) to be given, "the right hand of fellowship." Any major infraction like divorce landed you outside the church, or on the back row, excommunicated from "fellowship with the brethren." Under that framework, even though God's love was freely extended through the death of Jesus on the cross, it was not freely received. Believers felt that God's gift of salvation, though free, had to be "maintained" or "worked out" by your acts of service, devotion, and sacrifice. So, inadvertently, this belief system placed responsibility for your redemption, not exclusively on the finished works of Christ alone, but partly on your own efforts, and continuing good works.

I thought I was free from all that legalistic mindset when I left that denomination, grew up in faith, and understood the finished works of Christ. But, when I had the "major infraction" of divorce, those concepts, and associated wrong thinking from years ago came surging back, reinforced by the accusations of the enemy. This wrong mindset threatened to become a stronghold and for a long time, severely affected my attitude towards remarriage. I was single, but unavailable. I could hear the words of 1 Corinthians 7:10-11 playing over and over again in my mind, "But for those who are married, I have a command that comes not from me, but from the Lord. A wife must not leave her husband. But if she does leave him, let her remain single or else be reconciled to him." Since I did not want to be reconciled to my Ex, I chose to remain single.

I could not get over the words of apostle Paul, that this was a command "from the Lord". You see, I have built my entire life on the word of God. I treasure the word of God, and hold it in the highest esteem. It carries tremendous weight, and unquestionable authority with me. For me, the Bible is the infallible word of God and the final authority on all questions, issues, and discussions. If the word of God says so, that's enough for me. No debate, discussion or query. Both my ex-husband and the devil knew, and exploited my devotion to the word of God.

It took some doing over a long period of time, but once again, God came and delivered me from this stronghold. He stepped in, and by His grace spoke His love and truth again, and again, and again, until it pierced the darkness, bleakness, and despair of legalism. God's love healed me! Little by little, He untangled the web of wrong thinking. He showed me that while He hates divorce (Malachi 2:16), He loves me much, much, more, and that His grace redeems, and restores all the broken areas of our lives. Then He showed me in

Proverbs 6:16-19, the other things He hates: "These six *things* the LORD hates, Yes, seven *are* an abomination to Him: A proud look, A lying tongue, Hands that shed innocent blood, A heart that devises wicked plans, Feet that are swift in running to evil, A false witness *who* speaks lies, and one who sows discord among brethren." The Lord hates these seven things so much, that they are an abomination to him, yet He does not condemn the sinner. But the church has conveniently excused abominations like pride, lying, and gossip, and isolated divorce for elevated judgement, and special condemnation.

The Lord focused me on people like Joyce Meyer, Kenneth Copeland, and John Osteen (Joel Osteen's father), and others who are impacting the world, and living lives that honor God after a divorce. The Lord affirmed again, and again, that I needed to receive, believe, and hold onto His love without reservations or caveats. I had to stop allowing my circumstances to define me, or misinterpret the word of God to me. My identity was not in my marital status. If marriage did not qualify me, divorce cannot disqualify me. My identity was and is in Christ. God's word brought His love and truth to me, and the truth set me free. God's love healed me!

If marriage did not qualify me, divorce cannot disqualify me.

Looking back today, it is humbling to see how a mature Christian like myself can, in trying to be right, veer off into legalism, and become so wrong. Like James Macdonald once said, "If you are wrong in the way that you are right, then you are wrong even if you are right." I loved and treasured the word of God, but the devil twisted and distorted that allegiance into legalism. In trying to be right and obedient to the word of God, I took my eyes off Christ, and the grace and love of God, and focused on me, my actions, and circumstances. But the question is, if a perfect marriage without divorce could not qualify me for the love and grace of God, how can an imperfect marriage, with divorce disqualify me for the love and grace of God? Is the work of sin, and the devil more powerful that the work of Christ on the cross? Never!

4. Make Peace with Your Current Single Status: The next step to wholeness it to come to terms with your single status. Singleness by death or divorce is traumatic. It is a major loss – lost dreams, future, hopes and plans. Often, in their imagination, the newly single person is sitting on the floor in a pile of ashes. Everything is burned up by the pit fire of death or the raging forest fire of divorce, and nothing is left of the once beautiful life and story book future, except ashes. Sometimes relationship breakups can be equally devastating. In these scenarios, making peace with your current single status, looking yourself in the eye, and telling yourself the truth, and letting yourself know that it is okay not to be okay, is a very important step in the healing process.

In her book, On Death and Dying, Elizabeth Kubler Ross discussed five emotional stages that a person potentially goes through when facing the loss of a loved one. Ross's book has helped countless people make sense of the feelings that they experience after a painful loss. Even though this book has primary application to loss of a loved one through death, it has equal application to other types of loss, and in this case, loss of a spouse through divorce. In fact, depending on the circumstances, loss of a spouse through divorce can be even more emotionally damaging than loss through death, because loss through divorce often implicates the added trauma of betrayal, and severe emotional wounding intentionally inflicted by the person who was once beloved. So, while the person who is grieving the loss of a spouse through death can cling onto good memories for comfort, the person grieving the loss of a spouse through divorce is robbed even of that meager comfort.

Per Ross, the five emotional stages are chronologically: denial, anger, bargaining, depression, and acceptance. She explains that denial is a common defense mechanism that buffers the immediate shock of the loss, numbing us to our emotions. As the masking effects of denial and isolation begin to wear, reality and its pain re-emerge. But, we are not ready. So, the intense emotion is deflected from our vulnerable core, redirected, and expressed instead as anger. At the bargaining stage, we often have a feeling of guilt. This is the period where we go through a series of "If only" statements. We start to evaluate whether there was something we could have done differently to have helped save our loved one or our marriage. Depression is the fourth stage of grief. There are two types of depression that are associated with mourning. The first is a reaction to the practical implications of the loss. Sadness and regret predominate this type of depression. The second type of depression is more subtle and, in a sense, perhaps more private. It is our quiet preparation to separate and to bid our loved one or former spouse farewell. The fifth and final stage of grief is described by Kubler-Ross as acceptance. This phase is marked by withdrawal and calm *(Godson)*.

Coping with traumatic loss is ultimately a deeply personal and individual experience. Nobody can help you go through it easily or understand all the emotions you are experiencing. But, to move forward and be healed and whole again, you must not only go through the grieving process, you must get through it. You cannot remain in a perpetual state of grieving or get stuck in one of the first four stages, for example anger or depression. You must get to the fifth stage of grief – acceptance. You must accept, and make peace with your new single status.

Speaking the truth to yourself will help you to get up out of the ashes and re-engage life. Such truths as, "I am single and its okay"; "God loves me as much today as He did before my divorce"; "God still has a plan and purpose for my life"; "I cannot afford to fall apart, my children are depending on me"; "This will not destroy me, I will get through this"; and "There is life after divorce". Making peace with yourself as a single person grounds you in reality, helps you to accept your single status, and start to rebuild your life, and the lives of your children. It helps you to clear out the ashes, see what you have left over, and begin again. This is an extremely vulnerable time, when you need to step away, consolidate, reassess, establish a new normal, and tune-in to God to find our His plan for this season of your life. This is not a time to make big decisions!

Not making peace with your single status will set you up for bad, and sometimes self-destructive choices. For some people, failure to accept their singleness, coupled with anger, has caused them to seek new relationships too soon, without giving themselves the time to heal properly. They want to "show" their Ex, or do not want to be alone, or are afraid that they won't find someone else. So, they make reckless dating decisions, or compromise their moral convictions. Unfortunately, this behavior can lead to that one divorce or break-up becoming a cycle of disillusionment, and broken relationships. For others, lack of acceptance coupled with depression, makes them internalize the loss, devalue themselves, and offer themselves at a discount. They think they are "damaged goods", and nobody will want them, so they latch onto the next person that shows up. This wrong mindset sets them up to be taken advantage of, used, and abused. Others are afraid of the prospect of facing the future alone, and are financially insecure, so they rebound into dysfunctional relationships that end up being worse that the one they just came out of.

Jesus is the answer to loneliness, depression, financial lack, and fear of the future. Your new single status did not take Him by surprise. He has a plan for you, and for this season of your life. Trust Him, and take His hand. He will lead you through every emotional stage, and fill the gaps in your life. He will repair your vandalized foundation, and restore you to health, and wholeness. Simply stated, your way out is through, through Christ, and His word. Jesus is the resurrection, and the life. With Him, there is life after death, divorce, and relationship breakup.

My feelings are not the truth. They may be the facts, but they are not the truth. The word of God is the truth.

5. Immerse Yourself in The Word: An indispensable requirement for wholeness is staying full of God, and His word. God, our Father, has provided all that we need to win in our battle against the flesh, sin, the devil, and the world. The arsenal is in the word of God. The word is both our offensive, and defensive weapon against the enemy. It is both our sword, and shield. The word of God produces faith (Romans 10:17), which gives us victory over the world (1 John 5:4). Very importantly, the word of God renews our minds, it changes the way we think, and sets us free from wrong mindsets, and strongholds. It helps us to exchange our thoughts for God's thoughts. It compels us to see things from God's vantage point, and gives us God's perspective. It transforms us, and helps us to identify and distinguish between the good, acceptable, and perfect will of God (Romans 12:1-2).

The Word of God is the mirror for your spirit. In James 1:23-25, the Bible says:

> For if you listen to the word and don't obey,
> it is like glancing at your face in a mirror.
> You see yourself, walk away, and forget what
> you look like. But if you look carefully into
> the perfect law that sets you free, and if you
> do what it says and don't forget what you
> heard, then God will bless you for doing it.'

This scripture makes clear that the word of God is the mirror that shows, and describes to me in detail what my spirit looks like. It tells me who I am, what I have, and how I look in the spirit. Things exist in the spiritual world that I cannot see or feel except through the word of God. But when I believe the word, I release those things, and bring them into physical manifestation. If I believe the information from the "word mirror" and act on it, (the bible calls this faith), I will see change in the physical. How I feel is irrelevant. I just need to look in the spiritual mirror, believe what I see in it, and act on that information.

This is exactly what happens in the physical realm. The mirror shows me how I look physically, and I believe what I see in the mirror. If it tells me that my hair is out of order, and I take action to comb my hair in response to the mirror information, I will see the change. I don't "feel" that my hair is combed. I look at the mirror, believe what I see in the mirror and act accordingly.

Same thing in the spirit, it doesn't matter whether I feel sick, lonely, abandoned by God, or that my life is over. How I feel is irrelevant. I just need to look in the spiritual mirror - the word of God - believe what I see, and act on it. The word of God says that I am healed by the stripes of Jesus, (1 Peter 2:21-25); that I am a new creation in Christ, (2 Corinthians 5:17); that God will never leave me nor forsake me, (Hebrews 13:5), and that God has a great future planned for me, (Jeremiah 29:11). I must believe these truths, and act based on them. If I do, I release the power of God to change my circumstances. You see, my feelings are not the truth. They may be the facts, but they are not the truth. The word of God is the truth! When I believe what the word says, and act on it, I deploy the power, and grace of God to shut the door against sickness, loneliness, lack, and fear in my life. The truth of the word of God will always trump my feelings, and set me free to live the abundant life that Jesus died to give to me.

The state of your soul determines the course, direction, and outcomes of your life.

---

6. Guard Your Soul: Wholeness resides in the soul. So, to be whole, you must guard your soul. Your soul is the conduit between your spirit, and your body. A healthy soul allows the abundance, lavish resources, and nature of God located in our spirits to come through the bridge of our soul, and be manifested in, and through our bodies. Therefore, the state, and wellbeing of the soul has a direct correlation to the state, and wellbeing of the body. In 3 John 2, apostle John makes this connection when he states, "Beloved, I pray that you may prosper in all things and be in health, just as your soul prospers." This scripture is saying that a prosperous soul equals a prosperous life, and vice versa. This is why it is so critical to guard the soul. Proverbs 4:23 emphasizes this point even further. It states "Guard your heart above all else, for it determines the course of your life." Simply stated, the state of your soul determines the course, direction, and outcomes of your life.

As a Christian, my spirit is perfect, like Christ. But my soul is a work in progress. The word of God is the mirror that shows me what my spirit looks like, and in so doing, identifies the gap between my spirit and my soul. It shows me the difference between who I am in Christ, and who I am in practice. This gap analysis is very important to personal, and spiritual growth. It exposes me to my God-given potential, creates an awareness about my vulnerabilities, and produces a hunger in me to change to become what God created me to be.

My soul is made up of my mind - my thinker; my emotions - my feeler; and my will - my chooser. My soul is in the process of being redeemed, and the level of victory I experience in life, depends on the extent to which I engage in the transformation process described in Romans 12:2, "Don't copy the behavior and customs of this world, but let God transform you into a new person by changing the way you think. Then you will learn to know God's will for you, which is good and pleasing and perfect."

Mind: The mind is the battlefield, and victory or defeat starts with our thoughts. Proverbs 23:7 states that, "As a man thinks in his heart, so is he." Translation, the battle is won or lost between our ears. This is why God is very prescriptive about what we allow into our minds. The Bible tells us how to think, and what to think. First Corinthians 2:16 states that we have, "the mind of Christ". Philippians 4:8, instructs us to, "Fix your thoughts on what is true, and honorable, and right, and pure, and lovely, and admirable. Think about things that are excellent and worthy of praise." And Colossians 3:2 tells us to, "Think about the things of heaven, not the things of earth."

How can we do this? How can we win the battle of the mind? Proverbs 4:23 tells us how. It states, "Guard your heart above all else, for it determines the course of your life." To guard our hearts or souls, we must take control of our thoughts. We must guard our minds from enemy intrusion and takeover. We must stand watch over the access points or gateways into our mind – our eye gate, ear gate, and mouth gate. Make no mistake, what you watch on TV, what music you listen to, what books, and other material you read, what you say out of your mouth and the people you allow to speak into your life, will impact the texture and contours of your thought life. And whatever is on your mind will eventually come out through your mouth and actions. This is why king David, the man after God's heart prayed in Psalm 141:3, "Set a guard, O Lord, over my mouth; Keep watch over the door of my lips." Job had a similar commitment. In Job 31:1, he said, "I made a covenant with my eyes not to look with lust at a young woman." The message is simple. We cannot allow garbage into our minds and hope to live a life of victory. To be whole, we must take control of our thoughts, and to take control of our thoughts, we must beware what we allow to come in through our ear, eye, and mouth gates.

Emotions: In today's society, this is by far, the biggest danger zone in the soul. We live in a time and culture where emotions rule. They are fickle, fiery, and fleeting, but very powerful. For many people, their emotions are in the driver's seat of their lives. They are emphasized, exaggerated, and elevated to the status of truth. We have movies wholly dedicated to emotions, and emoticons have blossomed into a full-fledged industry. This extreme focus on emotions is aided and abetted by social media. People wear their emotions on their sleeve, and share even the deepest details of their lives with thousands of "friends" from around the world who they do not know. Each post boasts a generous sprinkling of emoticons. Life is all about feelings, and to most people, that is all the reality they know. The popular thinking is that feelings are uncontrollable. And since you cannot control how you feel, conventional wisdom dictates that you can say, do and act out exactly how, and what you feel. Doing anything different is viewed as being dishonest, lying to yourself or not being transparent. But that is not what the word of God teaches.

The Bible makes clear that we are not to be ruled, driven or controlled by our emotions, rather, we are to control them. God expects, and in fact, directs us not to live, act or react, based on how we feel, but to act, based on the word of God. Indeed, scripture teaches that spiritual maturity is a measure of our ability to rule over our emotions. In my book, *Choosing a Life of Victory*, I explain:

"A good indicator of whether or not you are a mature son or daughter is in your mind—how you think and what voice you follow. If you are ruled by your emotions, you are a child. If you cater to your flesh, you are a child. If you are led by your five senses, you are a child. If you know what is right to do but choose to act based on how you feel, you are a child" (*Godson*).

Will: This is your decision maker. It is the part of you that makes a choice whether or not to act. Your will is the seat of determination, perseverance, resolve, fortitude, execution, and follow through. Your thoughts drive your feelings, and your feelings place pressure on your will to act. This is the ultimate goal of the devil. It is the goal of advertisers too. They whip up your emotions, fill your mind with targeted information, and then bear down on your will, and drive you to take action based on that information. They yell, "This offer will not last long, pick up the phone and call now". Moving the will to act closes the sale and unfortunately, depending on the mover, and the action taken, can lead to a lifetime of sorrow, and destruction. Many a young man in jail today, some for life, were victims of emotionally driven action.

Connecting the dots between the mind, emotions, and will is critical, because it leads to character formation. Your thoughts produce emotions, your emotions activate, and move your will to make a choice, your choices form your habits, and your habits form your character, and ultimately, your destiny. This is why it is so important to take control of your thoughts, and stand guard over your eye, ear, and mouth gates.

7. Self-Definition: A critical link in the chain of wholeness is defining who you are, and aligning your self-definition with your source. Knowing your source gives you internal legitimacy, confident assurance, and personal authority. God is your source, so, you must be able to say to yourself and others with conviction, "I am from God". "He is my source of origin". "I am His image, and my self-definition come from Him alone". For a Christian single, this firm conviction and affirmation is foundational to wholeness.

If people's approval cannot define, validate or confirm me, then neither can their disapproval, rejection or ridicule invalidate or genuinely diminish me, unless I let it.

To be whole is to be restored to an unbroken, entire, undivided, full, and complete state. It is reconnecting with, and being comfortable with who you are at your core, and who God created you to be. It is seeing yourself through the eyes of your heavenly father, and drawing your sense of self from Him. It is recognizing and embracing the reality that in Christ, you are enough!

Genesis 1:26 states that God created us in His own image. Because I am from God, I do not need to be defined, affirmed, validated or confirmed by people, and should not look to people for approval. My self-definition, validation, personal authority, and affirmation come from my source - God. His approval does not depend on my works, looks, performance, meeting social conventions, or people's expectations. People are fickle, but God is not. He is constant, and His approval is unwavering. If people's approval cannot define, validate or confirm me, then neither can their disapproval, rejection or ridicule invalidate or genuinely diminish me, unless I let it. It has only the weight I ascribe to it, and I can elect to deprive it of any weight and power to hurt or negatively impact me. Even if the individual's express goal and intent was to diminish or neutralize me, I can refuse to be diminished, and in so doing completely rob their actions of power. This freedom from people is so important to godly self-definition and wholeness.

Jesus modeled this for us. He did not look to people for approval. In John 5:41 (NKJV), He said, "I do not receive honor from men." He did not try to convince people of His value or look to them to validate Him. He knew who He was! Jesus was free from people! Knowledge of who He was freed Him from human opinions, good or bad, and released Him to be all that God wanted Him to be.

For a Christian single, the path to wholeness is the path of freedom from the definition, approval, affirmation, and applause of people, and the world.

8. Personal Value: The ultimate goal of wholeness is to bring you to the place where you see yourself through the eyes of God. You are a son or daughter of Almighty God. Your value is not dependent on external factors like your looks, marital status, performance, who you know, your net worth, and so on. You belong to God and your personal value, authenticity, and authority flow from that relationship.

You are of inestimable value! If you ever question your personal value or doubt how God sees you, listen to what Max Lucado has to say:

"There are many reasons God saved you, to bring glory to himself, to appease his justice, to demonstrate his sovereignty. But one of the sweetest reasons God saved you, is because He is fond of you. He likes having you around. He thinks you are the best thing to come down the pike in quite a while. If God had a refrigerator, your picture will be on it. If He had a wallet, your photo will be in it. He sends you flowers every spring and a sunrise every morning. Whenever you want to talk, he'll listen. He can live anywhere in the universe and He chose your heart. Face it friend, He's crazy about you!"

To be whole, you must recognize and own your personal value. Whole singles are men and women of tremendous worth who value themselves, own their personal value, and are confident in themselves and their God. Whole singles value people, and treat all people with respect, because God values people.

Co-Dependency - The Relationship Lie

Our society has sold singles a bill of goods, and unfortunately, many singles have bought into the lie that if you are not married, engaged, in a relationship, or hooked up with someone, something is wrong with you. In fact, in today's sex-crazed culture, singleness is viewed in some circles as a handicap, and many single people are made to feel like they are defective in some way because they are not married. This feeling of marginalization is heightened by the fact that most churches are run by married people, and do not have a strong singles ministry. Some churches even discriminate against singles serving in some ministry roles. But this is all based on a big lie by the devil. The lie finds its root in the untruth that a single person is not complete, and that she or he needs another person to be complete or happy. This lie, plus the vocal expectations of family and friends, place immense pressure on single men and women to hurry into a relationship, even one that is not right for them, just so they can "have someone" or "be with someone". Unfortunately, this pressure often drives many Christian singles to desperation and into co-dependent relationships.

The Lost Self

Co-dependency has been referred to as the disease of the lost self. It is a dysfunctional relationship where one person supports or enables another person's wrongful behavior, such as addiction, immaturity, irresponsibility, and so forth. The most common theme of co-dependency is an excessive reliance on other people for approval and a sense of identity. A codependent person is someone who cannot function from his or her innate self, and who's thinking or behavior is organized around another person or a process or substance.

Common symptoms of codependency include:

a. Intense and unstable interpersonal relationships

b. Inability to tolerate being alone, accompanied by frantic efforts to avoid being alone.

c. Chronic feelings of boredom and emptiness

d. Subordinating one's own needs to those of the person with whom one is involved

e. Overwhelming desire for acceptance and affection

f. Low self-worth

g. Overcontrolling, manipulation, and perfectionism

h. Unhealthy clinginess where one person does not have self-sufficiency or personal autonomy

Breaking the Cycle of Co-Dependency - Exposing the Lie

The premise of co-dependency - needing someone else to the point that you compromise, sacrifice, subsume yourself or lose your personal autonomy just to be with them - is a lie. The truth is that you can live a full, fulfilled, and successful adult life as a single man or woman. "Single adults in the Bible demonstrate that the single life is both a viable option and one that affords people the opportunity to live uniquely for the Lord– undistracted by particular concerns of the world" *(Dr. David Hoffeditz, "They Were Single Too).* God affirms every individual, single or married, as a person of tremendous worth and value, with a God-given purpose, future, and destiny. His plan is for every single person to live a life filled with His presence, purpose, passion, and power.

So many Bible characters were single at various times in their lives, and some, for all of their lives. Adam was single until God created Eve, Miriam was single all her life, Ruth and Naomi were both single after their husbands died. Jeremiah was single his entire life, Nehemiah was single, Joseph was single until he was in his thirty's, Daniel and his friends, Shadrach, Meshack and Abednego were single all their lives. John the Baptist was single all his life. Apostle Paul was single all his life. Martha was single. Anna became a widow after only 7 years of marriage, and remained single the rest of her life, Lydia was a single business woman, and the list goes on and on.

You will recognize these names as men and women who achieved tremendous things for the kingdom of God, lived whole lives, and left a huge footprint on planet earth. Two of my heroes in the Bible deserve special mention. They lived their entire lives on earth as single men, and they changed the world! How did they do it? They knew who they were, had a very strong sense of purpose, and mission, and valued their singleness. My first single hero is Jesus. He lived on this earth for thirty-three years as a single man. Today, a man who is thirty-three and not married or in a relationship, is viewed by society as a misfit. He is seen as "having no game", and pressured by the culture to "play the field". This view point is certainly not of God! It is straight from the pit of hell, and is a strategy by the devil to wreak havoc in the lives of people. Jesus lived a full and complete life. He started his ministry at age thirty, as a single man, and He changed the world.

Apostle Paul, my second single hero, chose a life of singleness and liked it so much that he recommends that lifestyle to others. In 1 Corinthians 7:7 he states, "For I wish that all men were even as I myself." He continued in verse 8, "I say to the unmarried and to the widows; it is good for them if they remain even as I am." In verse

32-33, he explains why. "I want you to be without care. He who is unmarried cares for the things of the Lord – how he may please the Lord. But he who is married cares about the things of the world – how he may please his wife". Paul lived a full and complete life as a single man and He changed the world. Next to Jesus, no other man had a more profound impact on the history of the early church as apostle Paul. He evangelized the known world of his time and wrote most of the new testament. And he accomplished all this as a single man.

My third hero is not from the Bible. He is Dr. Charles Stanley, senior pastor of First Baptist Church in Atlanta, Georgia, and founder of In Touch Ministries. He was divorced by his wife Anna in 2000 and has been single since then. He is not sitting around moping and feeling sorry for himself. Instead, he is living a full and fulfilled life as a Christian minister. He has a worldwide ministry that is reaching millions daily. He has written so many books, and left a rich legacy of faithful, and diligent service to the Lord. He loves photography and has produced amazing works that thrill the eyes, and bless the hearts of people.

These examples illustrate the point that every Christian single can live a life of impact and tremendous fruitfulness, not tomorrow, or when they get married, but today, right where they are. So, stop pining and start living!

Is Jesus Enough for You?

I cannot end this chapter on wholeness without asking you a question, a deeply personal question, "Is Jesus enough for you?" This question is critical to wholeness because you will NEVER be whole until Jesus is enough for you. Unfortunately for many singles, Jesus is not enough. Now, they don't say that verbally, but it is clear from their actions and pre-occupation. For some, it is Jesus plus a child, for others it is Jesus plus a husband or wife. What they don't realize is that nothing will be enough, until Jesus is enough.

When Jesus is enough, then you are released from the obsession to be married, be in a relationship, or meet other people's expectations or definition of social status. When Jesus is enough, you are no longer embarrassed to be single, or avoid social gatherings, and family reunions because you don't have a "plus one". This does not mean that you no longer desire to be married or that you choose a lifetime of singleness. But it does mean that you can rest, and trust God with this single season of your life. Declaring that Jesus is enough helps you to shut down your "DIY" (Do It Yourself) operation. It keeps you from fenagling your way, "manufacturing" your miracle, or birthing an "Ishmael"; which simply means trying to "help God out", by attempting to achieve God's plans and purposes through works of the flesh (Genesis 16).

Is Jesus enough when His answer to your prayer is no? Is He enough when He says "wait"? Is He enough when you are pushing 40 and are still single? Is He enough when the relationship you thought would lead to marriage just broke up and you are devastated? Is He enough when your biological clock is ticking away and taking your desire to have kids along with it? Is Jesus enough for you in every season of your life? To be whole, you must decide to speak to your soul, and conclusively affirm that Jesus is enough for you; on the mountain-tops, and the valleys, when you are lonely, feeling depressed or discouraged.

I am not talking about a stoic resignation to "your fate" or a resentful withdrawal. Nor am I talking about simply settling for the status quo. What I am talking about is a quiet resolve that nestles in the depths of your soul. A peace born out of trust in the goodness and fatherhood of God. It is a recognition that our God is Alpha and Omega, the beginning, and the end. He is the Lord of time and has your times in His hands. It is a willing submission to, not only His plan, but His process, and timing too. It is a surrender of your prefer-ences, timelines, expectations, and dreams to Jehovah-nick-of-time and a calm, and sober trust that even if He delays by your timeline, He will never be late. He will be there in the nick of time. It is a settled content-ment, and confident assurance in the plans, purposes, methods, and timing of God.

Your position should be, "Lord, I do not want any-thing or anyone in my life that you did not give to me". There is a practical reason for this. Anything or anyone that you get without the Lord, you will eventually lose. So, hurrying into a relationship or marriage outside of God's will and timing is looking for trouble. The relationship will not last. Eventually you will have two options, divorce, in which case you will not only be single again, but now you are scarred and marred by the tragedy of the failed first marriage; or you choose to stay in a bad relationship and settle for way beneath your inheritance.

I think of my life as a home that God has built and furnished for himself. Every piece of "furniture" is hand selected by him and bears his imprimatur. Having a husband or relationship in my life that I did not receive from the Lord will not match the décor of my life. It will be out of place, and out of synch with the overall theme of my life, which is Christ, and Christ alone.

Nothing will be enough until Jesus is enough. Single or married, you will never be whole until Jesus is enough for you.

Single or married, you will never find purpose, fulfillment, and wholeness until Jesus is enough for you.

CHAPTER 2

WELL

THERE ARE MANY GOOD WORDS THAT BEGIN with W. Words like wealthy, witty, wise, warm, wholesome, winner, and so on. But no other W word captures the essence of wholeness for a Christian single like the word well. This is first because "well" embodies and encompasses all the other words, and secondly, it is a powerful prefix. When placed before almost any other word, it can turn it into a positive and empowering word. Examples abound, including: well-made, well-spoken, well-behaved, well-adjusted, well-done; and so on. This is exactly what whole singles do, they always add value to any environment in which they engage. Whole singles are well singles.

Whole singles are well singles.

During my separation and divorce, I began a saying that has stayed with me and become part of my private lexicon. I decided, right in the middle of all the mess, that whenever anyone asked me how I was doing, I would simply respond, "It is well with my soul". This was my pre-determined response regardless of how I felt or what was going on around me at the time. I determined that I was not going to complain, whine or bemoan my fate. Rather, I would make that simple declaration over my life. I took those words from Isaiah 3:10 that states, "Tell the godly, that all will be well for them", and the popular hymn with that title by Horatio Spafford. Every day, in response to "How are you?" inquiries from friends and co-workers, instead of saying, "fine" or complaining, I would say, "It is well with my soul". In a typical day, I would make that declaration several times, and it kept my spirit tenacious, and my mind focused on the promises of God, so that I was not overwhelmed by my circumstances. In fact, that saying became so much a part of me, that it has been associated with me ever since. This last Christmas, more than a decade later, two friends gave me Christmas gifts with the inscription, "It is well with my soul". That declaration of wellness was a healing balm to my soul and looking back, everything has turned out well for me and my children.

"Well" is a word that refers to every aspect of a person's being. As an adverb, it means good, satisfactory or thorough. As an adjective it means healthy, fit, fine, strong, thriving, vigorous, and free or recovered from illness. It also means sensible, prudent, advantageous, beneficial, profitable, desirable, and wise. Further, well is often used as an exclamation to express a range of emotions including surprise, anger, resignation, or relief. In other words, "well" can apply to or describe the state of our emotions, mind, will, and body. What a word!

---

*How beautiful or handsome are you
on the inside?*

"Well" is a key step and requirement for wholeness in the spirit, soul, and body. Our born again spirit is well, because it is the only part of us that is perfect. Since our spirit is well, complete, and settled in God, that perfect condition of our spirits can be carried over the bridge of our souls to manifest in our body or in the physical realm. This can happen in reference to a particular issue, situation or circumstance, such that we are well in mind and soul about that specific situation. It can also be a generalized, more durable state of wellbeing, where there is an overall and enduring "wellness" in our mind, and soul. This prevailing state of established and ongoing "wellness" is where we want to get to. A place where we are not moved by what we see, hear or by our circumstances. Rather, our state of wellbeing is dependent on a transcendent perspective and understanding, grounded in the person, character, and purposes of God.

Wellness speaks of inner beauty, the beauty of a gentle and quiet spirit, a soul that is secure and at rest.

A well person is always more beautiful or handsome on the inside than they are on the outside. That inner beauty comes from a close relationship with Christ, a clear understanding of who they are in Him, and their value in God's eyes. That exuberant confidence, strength, and poise radiates out from their well souls, and permeates all their interactions.

First Peter 3:3-4 admonishes godly women:

> Don't be concerned about the outward beauty of fancy hairstyles, expensive jewelry, or beautiful clothes. You should clothe yourselves instead with the beauty that comes from within, the unfading beauty of a gentle and quiet spirit, which is so precious to God.

My question to you is, how beautiful or handsome are you on the inside?

There is no wholeness without wellness. As discussed earlier, wholeness resides in the soul, which is the seat of our mind, emotions, and will. The soul space can be tumultuous. It is the arena of battle for control of our lives. Our born again spirit is perfect and indwelt by the Holy Spirit. Romans 8:16 confirms this truth. It states, "For His Spirit joins with our spirit to affirm that we are God's children". However, our bodies are earth bound, and before we were saved, was conditioned to living according to the dictates of this world.

Our souls catered to our bodies and was conformed to the pattern of this world, until we gave our lives to Christ. Then the conflict erupted! Going forward, when our body wants to do things the way it is accustomed to doing them, the Holy Spirit intervenes and imparts the word and will of God about the situation to our soul. Our bodies rebel against what it considers an imposition or undue restraint by the Holy Spirit. It wants and likes "business as usual", and resents the constraining and moderating influence of the Holy Spirit.

Now the soul is in a quandary. It is accustomed to acting based on the information it receives from the body and its five senses; but now there is a new sheriff in town; the Holy Spirit; with a strong urging to do things differently, and deep inside; the soul knows that the Spirit's direction is right, but it is bullied by the body's whining, harassed by bombarding thoughts, and pressured by the feelings which those thoughts unleash, to cave in to the demands of the body.

In Galatians 5:17, the Bible describes this raging warfare: "The sinful nature wants to do evil, which is just the opposite of what the Spirit wants. And the Spirit gives us desires that are the opposite of what the sinful nature desires. These two forces are constantly fighting each other, so you are not free to carry out your good intentions." Even apostle Paul was not immune to this. In Romans 7:18-19, he gives us a glimpse of this ongoing battle in his own life. He states: "And I know that nothing good lives in me, that is, in my sinful nature. I want to do what is right, but I can't. I want to do what is good, but I don't. I don't want to do what is wrong, but I do it anyway."

Given this ongoing battle in the soul, it is possible to walk in victory? The answer is a resounding yes, but it is not something that we can achieve in our own ability. It is the work of the Holy Spirit in our lives. Victory is sure when we yield to the Holy Spirit's leading. We see an example in the life of Christ. In the garden of Gethsemane, with the trauma of the cross looming large, His flesh and the devil mounted a major onslaught to keep Him from going to the cross. They pressured Him to exercise His human will to walk away from the cross. The bible described the intense confrontation and agony in Luke 22:41-44:

> He walked away, about a stone's throw, and knelt down and prayed, "Father, if you are willing, please take this cup of suffering away from me. Yet I want your will to be done, not mine." Then an angel from heaven appeared and strengthened him. He prayed more fervently, and he was in such agony of spirit that his sweat fell to the ground like great drops of blood.

The battle was raging! Jesus could have caved in to His flesh and walked away from the cross. He could have saved Himself, but then He would have aborted the mission, because He cannot save Himself and us at the same time, so He chose us. After his intense agony and tears, He quieted His soul and brought it under the control of the Spirit. A quiet calm settled over Him, a deep resolve to do the father's will. His emotions were no longer in charge, the Spirit was. He knew what He had to do, and He was ready. This transformation was so complete that when the crowd came with Judas to arrest Him, He was in such firm control of His emotions that He spoke calmly to Judas, instructed the disciples to show restraint, healed the ear of Malchus that was lopped off by Peter, and calmly asked the high priest and his posse questions, all without any outward display of overt emotion. His mind was made up, His soul was subdued, and the Spirit ruled. At that time, it was well with Jesus's soul, not because God had removed the cross, but because He gave Him the fortitude to endure and overcome it.

What is a Well Soul?

A well soul is a soul at rest. A soul with undivided trust and confidence in God. A soul that is stable, solid, steadfast, and immovable. A well soul is a soul that is abandoned to God, has entrusted the ups and downs of life into the loving hands of Almighty God, and is content with the outcome, even when it is unpleasant, and does not match its expectations. A well soul is a soul that has tears in the eyes but unflinching confidence in the heart. A well soul is a soul that is unperturbed by circumstances and that is fixed on God with an undivided heart. One word to describe a well soul is peace.

The Bible speaks a lot about peace. Lack of peace is a condition where a person is agitated, troubled, disturbed, fearful, or unsettled. Peace on the other hand is a quiet restfulness, a steady and unwavering resolve to confront challenging circumstances with faith, fortitude, and grace. Isaiah 9:6 calls Jesus the Prince of peace. And in John 14:27, Jesus said; "Peace I leave with you; my peace I now give and bequeath to you. Not as the world gives do I give to you. Do not let your hearts be troubled, neither let them be afraid." This scripture outlines the following truths:

1. **I Already Have and Possess Peace:** Jesus gave me His peace. So, I already possess the ability to have established and ongoing wellbeing in my soul. Right now, despite my circumstances, I have peace and it is well with my soul, because Jesus gave and bequeathed His peace to me.

2. **Jesus's Peace Vs the World's Peace:** Jesus makes a distinction between His peace and the peace of the world. So, the world does have peace, but its peace is unlike the peace that Jesus gives. The world's peace is dependent on circumstances and controlling our outcomes to meet our expectations. The world's peace makes human sense. But the peace

of God passes all understanding, meaning that it does not make human sense. It is a peace like Jesus had when He was sleeping in the midst of the storm (Mark 4:39). It is the kind of peace that Peter had, when he was sleeping in jail, waiting to be executed the next day (Acts 12:3-19). This is the peace that looks trouble in the eye with a steady, steadfast, and unflinching gaze of faith and trust in the name, character, and grace of Almighty God.

3. **I Am the Custodian of My Peace:** It is my responsibility to guard my peace, because I can keep or lose it. The Amplified version makes this clear. It translates John 14:27 as follows: "Stop allowing yourselves to be agitated and disturbed; and do not permit yourselves to be fearful and intimidated and cowardly and unsettled". Simply stated, I am the custodian of my peace, and by implication, wellness in my soul. I can choose to not be agitated, troubled, perturbed, and so on, or I can choose to "allow or permit myself to be agitated, perturbed, and so forth.

These truths are the opposite of what most people think, and certainly very different from the lie that our society peddles; the lie that our feelings are free agents that have a mind of their own, and there is nothing we can do to restrain them. By contrast, the Bible makes us responsible and holds us accountable for allowing fear, agitation, and perturbation into our hearts. We are the gate keepers. We can choose our feelings and we can choose to act differently from how we feel.

WHOLE Singles Take Charge of Their Emotions

Wholeness requires that we take charge of our emotions. We have the ability and power to choose how we feel and how we act. We can choose to shut down negative feelings and substitute them with positive feelings. All it entails is maturity and growth in the soul. There is a misconception, that ruling over our emotions is being dishonest or inauthentic. But that is a lie. In the above example of Jesus in the garden of Gethsemane, He prayed passionately and wept desperately in His private time with the Father. But after that, He arose with a deep resolve and strength to face the cross. It does not mean that He felt no fear, or suddenly felt happy about his impending crucifixion. Not at all. His flesh still wanted Him to turn and run, but instead, He moved forward with intentionality and driven by purpose. He did not act based on how He felt. He took charge of His emotions, and acted in keeping with the word of God.

It is clear from His example that "well" does not mean perfect or a life free from challenges. Well people don't have it all together. In fact, it is the state of being well in adverse circumstances that distinguishes the peace of God from the peace of the world. This is what Jesus meant when He said, "I have told you all this so that you may have peace in me. Here on earth you will have many trials and sorrows. But be of good cheer, because I have overcome the world" (John 16:33). On the one hand Jesus says, "you will have many trials and sorrows", and on the other He says, "be of good cheer". This looks like an oxymoron. The only way to reconcile these two apparent contradictions, is peace, His peace. And He modeled this for us in the garden of Gethsemane. It is Jesus's ability to look His would be murderers in the eye and calmly talk to one and heal the ear of another, that sets Him apart from the world.

"It is well with my soul" is a popular hymn written by Horatio Spafford and composed by Philip Blass. The hymn was written after traumatic events in Spafford's life. The first was the death of his only son at the age of two and the great Chicago fire of 1871, which ruined him financially. He had been a successful lawyer and had invested heavily in property along Lake Michigan's shoreline, an area extensively damaged by the fire. His business interests were further devastated by the economic downturn of 1873, at which time he planned to travel to Europe with his family. In a last minute change of plans, he sent his family ahead while he was delayed on business concerning zoning problems following the great Chicago fire. While crossing the Atlantic Ocean, the ship carrying his family collided with another vessel and all of Spafford's four daughters died. His wife Anna survived, and sent him the now famous telegram, "Saved alone...". Shortly afterwards, Spafford traveled to meet

his grieving wife. When the ship passed near the spot where his daughters had died, the captain informed the grieving Spafford, who went to his cabin and wrote the words of this dear hymn. Looking at Spafford's circumstances, which paralleled that of Job in the bible, "It is well with my soul" sounds like a cruel joke, but it was not. It is the truth that in the midst of life's tragedies, there is a peace, faith, and hope that transcends life's circumstances, that can only be found in Christ. This is why this hymn has endured the test of time and blessed countless generations.

Second Kings 4:8 tells the story of a "great woman", the woman of Shunem. She was a wealthy woman who took it upon herself to care for and support Elisha the prophet of God. So, she built an addition to her home to provide guest quarters for the prophet. She simply wanted to minister to him, but as always happens, God blessed her beyond her dreams. The man of God found out that she had no child, so he prophesied to her, "Next year at this time you will be holding a son in your arms!" "No, my lord!" she cried. "O man of God, don't deceive me and get my hopes up like that." But sure enough, the woman soon became pregnant, and at that time the following year she had a son, just as Elisha had said" (2 Kings 4: 16-17).

One day, while the boy was out with his father in the field, he had what appears to be a heat stroke. His father sent him home to his mother. He sat on her lap until noon and died. The Bible describes what happens next.

"And she went up and laid him on the bed of the man of God, shut *the door* upon him, and went out. Then she called to her husband, and said, "Please send me one of the young men and one of the donkeys, that I may run to the man of God and come back." So he said, "Why are you going to him today? *It is* neither the New Moon nor the Sabbath." And she said, "*It is* well" (2 Kings 4:21-23)

Think about that! Her only child had just died, a child that she had conceived against incredible odds. The Bible indicates that she had been childless for a while and her husband was old. The fact that she has lost all hope of having a child is evident in her response to Elisha when he told her that she would conceive. She said to him, "O man of God, don't deceive me and get my hopes up like that." So, having this child was a miracle and there was no real prospect of her having another child. Plus, the fact that the boy had died suddenly. There is no indication in the scripture that he had been sick. The bible just states that:

"He went out to help his father, who was working with the harvesters. Suddenly he cried out, "My head hurts! My head hurts!" His father said to one of the servants, "Carry him home to his mother." So the servant took him home, and his mother held him on her lap. But around noontime he died."

His death was sudden and traumatic. Most women would collapse and cry hysterically, but not this woman. Make no mistake. She was as distraught as any mother would be who lost her only child unexpectedly and in such tragic circumstances, but instead of falling apart, she reined in her emotions and sprang into action. She did not even tell her husband what had happened and when asked, she said, "It is well". This woman went looking for Elisha the man of God. When Elisha saw her, he knew something was horribly wrong. He sent Gehazi his servant to meet her. He said: "Please run now to meet her, and say to her, '*Is it* well with you? *Is it* well with your husband? *Is it* well with the child?'" And she answered, "*It is* well." This woman was unwavering in her confidence that God will intervene on her behalf and raise her son from death, and He did.

"It is well" is not a statement for wimps. It is not a wishy washy cliché. It is a statement rooted in a firm conviction that the God of heaven is a good God, and that He is who He says that He is, and will do exactly what He says that He will do. It is a statement that flows from a heart that is not ruled by emotions, but that is rested and nested in God. As I shared earlier, "It is well with my soul" was my personal battle cry during the toughest times of my life.

Ships are made for the ocean. It is their natural habitat. A ship's intended destiny is to sail the high seas. It is built specifically to perform successfully in the water. So, a ship is not threatened by water. For a ship, being in the water or surrounded by water is perfectly normal, and the ship is fine and dandy to be in the midst of all the water in the world, as long as it stays on top of the water. The ship gets into trouble when the water on the outside, gets into the ship. The ship can sail mighty oceans and be unscathed, but a relatively small amount of water inside the ship can completely destroy it.

> *Make God your primary focus, and you will be at peace. Make the world your primary focus, and you will be in pieces.*

It is the same thing with us as human beings and as Christians. Jesus said, "In the world you will have trouble". It's a promise, though not the kind that we would like to claim. So, having trouble in this world is not unusual. Jesus had a boat load of trouble himself. We are built strong, sturdy, and resilient to withstand life's storms. Like the ship, our maker prepared and equipped us to sail in life's turbulent seas without drowning or being overrun. But that is only as long as we don't allow the outside trouble to get into our souls. Like the ship, we get into trouble when we let the outside storm get inside our heads and heart. That is why the Bible tells us to watch over our souls with diligence. This is also why the devil aggressively targets our souls. We must be diligent, intentional and deliberate to plug any holes in our lives that would compromise our ability to stay afloat, and maintain a well soul in the midst of life's challenges.

How Can You Have a "Well" Soul?

1. **Keep Your Mind on Christ:** Isaiah 26:3 tells us that it is all about focus. Your focus determines your mindset and the condition of your soul. Make God your primary focus, and you will be at peace. Make the world your primary focus and you will be in pieces. How do you make God your primary focus? Fix your thoughts on Him. Think, speak, listen to, and meditate on His word. Isaiah 26:3 states that God will keep in perfect peace all who trust in Him, all whose thoughts are fixed on Him. Then it admonishes us to trust in the Lord always, because He is the eternal rock. In today's world where everything is slipping and sliding – values, morals, financial markets, and standards - keeping our eyes and thoughts on God will help us maintain a "well" soul, a soul that is not tossing and turning with every sound bite from CNN, or other news media outlets. A soul that knows that regardless of what is happening in the world, God is on His throne and His kingdom rules over all.

2. **Prayer:** The Bible states pointedly that prayer is an antidote to worry and anxiety, two major contraindicators of a well soul. Simply stated, prayer, with thanksgiving is a peace facilitator. Philippians 4:4-7 states:

"Don't worry about anything; instead, pray about everything. Tell God what you need, and thank him for all he has done. Then you will experience God's peace, which exceeds anything we can understand. His peace will guard your hearts and minds as you live in Christ Jesus."

This scripture establishes a cause and effect relationship between prayer, thanksgiving and peace, God's kind of peace. This means that if you will pray about your problem with a thankful heart, peace is the inevitable result. What is more, contrary to how most people think about peace, it tells us that God's kind of peace is not a feeling. It is a soldier, an armed guard on assignment, commissioned to mount guard over your soul and ensure that it is well, regardless of your circumstances. Peace would ward off intruders, like the negative voices of the devil and other people; as well as intercept and neutralize interlopers like "what if" thoughts, and thoughts of worry and anxiety. Also, peace would alert you to oncoming danger, like negative traffic from the TV, people headed your way with an assignment from hell to frustrate and distract you, any incoming missiles from the devil, and fiery darts of discouragement, disappointment, and disillusionment.

Prayer is a peace facilitator.

3. **Renew Your Mind:** We have already learned that the battlefield is in the theatre of our minds and that we win or lose the battle in that arena. So, Romans 12:2 gives us a strategy focused on the mind and a road map to victory. It tells us that the only way to win the battle is to renew our minds. What this means is that we exchange our thoughts and opinions for God's thoughts and opinions. Isaiah 55:8 states that God's thoughts are higher than our thoughts and His ways are higher than our ways. However, God has made His thoughts and ways readily available to us in the Bible. So how can we exchange our thoughts for God's thoughts? By learning God's thoughts from the Bible and applying what He says to our circumstances. The process is simple. Study the Bible, accept what it says as the infallible word of God and the final authority on all questions, issues and discussions, and then do what the Bible says. Romans 12:2 states that if we do this, our minds will be renewed or repro-gramed with God's thoughts and perspectives. This renewal process will transform us, and equip us to know, and recognize what the will of God is, His good, acceptable, and perfect will.

4. **Permit/Allow Peace to Rule as an Umpire**: God rules in our hearts and guides our affairs through His peace. This peace is His unique stamp that helps us to identify God's plan, confirm His approval, and

decide between competing interests. Colossians 3:15, instructs every believer to "Let the peace that comes from Christ rule in your hearts". This scripture emphasizes that we have control over the state of our soul, and directs us to put peace in charge! We must let peace, the peace that comes from Christ, referee issues in our lives and call the balls and strikes, like an umpire. It makes the point that not all "peace" comes from Christ. There is a false "peace" that comes from conforming to the world's system, going along to get along, being a people pleaser or from favorable circumstances. When we put the peace that comes from Christ in charge of our lives, allow it to take the lead in decision making, and establish God's rule in our hearts, we would have a well soul.

God's peace is a soldier, an armed guard on assignment, commissioned to mount guard over your soul and ensure that it is well, regardless of your circumstances.

---

5. **Faith in the Character and Word of God:** Knowledge of and faith in the character of God is a strong soul stabilizer. It is the impenetrable trust born of an unshakable conviction that our heavenly father sees us where we are and is deeply involved in all the details of our lives. It is a faith built on

the solid foundation of the immutability of God's character, person, and word. God cannot change (Malachi 3:6); God cannot lie (Titus 1:2); God does not vacillate, and change His mind like human beings (Numbers 23:19). God can be safely trusted. He is all wise, Almighty, omnipotent, omniscient, omnipresent, good, and faithful.

The popular saying that "the devil is in the details" is not true for a Christian. For every son or daughter of God, our heavenly father is involved in the details of our lives. Knowledge of that truth anchors our hearts in the midst of the storms of life. When life doesn't make sense, we can say, "Right now, I don't understand and can't explain what God is doing in my life, but I trust Him. I know that He is working on my behalf. Somehow, He will make all this work together for my good" *(Godson)*. Job modeled this truth so powerfully. Even though he lost everything, his children, wealth and health, literally overnight, he said: "Though He slay me, yet will I trust Him" (Job 13:15).

This is the resolute assurance that in Christ, we win, no matter what happens! We may lose things, possessions, relationships, positions, or life itself. But when it's all said and done, we win. It is a confidence based on the understanding that the president is not in charge, congress is not in charge, the democrats are not in charge, the republicans are not in charge, and the devil is not in charge. God Almighty is in charge. Isaiah 33:22 articulates it clearly, "For the Lord is our judge, the Lord is our lawgiver, the Lord is our king; it is he who will care for us and save us". This scripture is a wake-up call for those who are trying to make the government their God and provider. Our God is Lord over the judicial, legislative, and executive arms of government, and only He can help us. Psalm 62:11 sums it up in four words, "power belongs to God". This truth should minister peace to your heart. God is our King, we are plugged into His kingdom, and the laws of the kingdom of God governs our lives and affairs. This knowledge produces faith and freedom from fear, worry or anxiety about the future. It produces peace and wellness in the soul.

6. **Praise:** Praise and worship is a soul lubricant. It causes the soul to bask in the radiant sunshine of God's presence and to gaze into His glorious face. Praise is one of the most transcendent activities we can engage in. It elevates our vision and thinking above the challenges and problems that want to keep us earth bound, and enables us to soar without limitations. Praise unhitches our arms, legs, and neck from the burdens, yokes, and weights that hold us down and we can lift off to heights of unlimited ecstasy where we see our God as bigger than all our problems, bigger than all our fears, bigger

than any mountain, any challenge, situation or circumstance. Praise assures our hearts that God is for us. It tells the devil that we believe God, no matter what. Praise empowers us to see our situation through God's eyes, and fixing our gaze on Him cuts our problems down to size. It's like the hymn writer Helen Howarth Lemmel wrote:

"Turn your eyes upon Jesus
Look full in His wonderful face
And the things of earth will grow strangely dim
In the light of His glory and grace

7. **Break Curses and Satanic Covenants:** Renouncing, and breaking curses, and other demonic entanglements is a critical piece in ensuring a well soul that is free from bondage and oppression. This is because most oppression is caused by demonic traffic and activity. Several times in the Bible, Jesus addressed sicknesses and other forms of bondage by casting out a demonic spirit, and once the demon leaves, so does the condition that it fostered, maintain, and supervised. There are demonic forces that are deployed by the devil to maintain specific dysfunctions in the life of a person or family. These are sometimes called familiar spirits, and the condition that they engender is called generational curses. Generational curses are impediments, disadvantages, or problems that run in a family from

one generation to the next. They can manifest as a recurring failure, sin, character flaw, calamity that befalls that family, and so on. They can also be strongholds of the mind, thought patterns, habits, and emotional bondage. An example of a generational curse placed on a person in the Bible, is in 2 Samuel 3:29. As a Christian, you have the right and authority to terminate any curse, drown every voice speaking from your past and ancestry, shut down the operation of the wicked spirits supervising and enforcing the curse or dysfunction in your life, and deliver yourself to walk in glorious freedom in Christ.

The place to start is to believe what the word of God says. John 8:36 states that Jesus has set us free, and whom the Son sets free, is free indeed. Numbers 23:19 states that we are blessed, and cannot be cursed, and our blessing is irreversible! Galatians 3:13-14 says that Jesus redeemed us from the curse of the law, and became a curse for us, so that we don't have to live under any curse, but rather, we inherit the blessings of Abraham. This means that, not only did God redeem us from the curse, He set up generational blessings for us. Abraham's blessings are ours. This is a liberating truth, but it must be activated. When a person becomes a Christian, they are deputized by Jesus to exercise their authority, to break any and every curse operating in their lives and family

How to Break Curses and Demonic Covenants

1. Repent of any sin on your part that opened the door to the curse or demonic covenant to operate in your life.

2. Forgive anyone who sinned against you.

3. Declare that you belong to God, and are bought with the precious blood of Jesus.

4. Renounce every association with the occult. Repent of every way that you opened the door to demonic traffic in your life, and shut the door on the devil.

5. Cancel every negative word that anyone spoke over you, and revoke every license you granted to the wrong people to speak into your life.

6. Destroy any tokens such as artifacts, images, carvings, souvenirs, gifts, or "family heirloom", received or connected with the curse or covenant.

7. Revoke every curse or demonic covenant operating in your life. Declare Galatians 3:13 - Jesus redeemed you from the curse by becoming a curse for you.

8. Bind the strongman familiar spirit, and the strongman spirit of bondage, and cast them out of

your life (Matthew 12:29). Loose the Holy Spirit, the Spirit of liberty, adoption, and sonship.

9. Bind the wicked spirits sent by the devil and his strongmen to supervise and enforce the curse in your life. Terminate their assignment, shut down their operation, and cast them out.

10. Declare your freedom and wholeness in Christ, because whom the Son sets free is free indeed. Proclaim Galatians 5:1. Jesus set you free from every curse or satanic covenant. You refuse to be bound!

11. Declare that you belong to the lineage of Christ, and that the blood of Jesus is your bloodline. Silence any voice speaking against you from your past or ancestry, because Jesus has completely destroyed them.

12. Take communion, to declare your union with Christ and deliverance from the devil and his kingdom.

8. The Spoken Word: Speaking the word of God from your mouth will establish wellness in every area of your life. The W ord of God is a bag of seed (Matthew 13:1-23). If there is any area of your life that is unwell, find the word of God that addresses that situation, and plant it in the soil of your heart. How do you plant the word? By speaking it forth in faith. The promises of God are voice activated. So, to have a well soul, cultivate the word of God in your life and launch it forth daily through the spoken word. "The Word of God coming out of my mouth, in faith, is the most potent weapon known to man. What this means, is that every word I speak is on assignment. Once I believe the Word in my heart and launch it forth via the spoken word, it will not return empty; it will achieve its creative purpose and assignment. It is unstoppable!" (Godson).

The promises of God are voice activated.

'Well" also describes physical wellbeing, but we will cover that in the next chapter.

Enemies of Wellness

1. Reproach, Shame, and Stigma: These are the triple evil sisters of the devil. A reproach is an <u>expression</u> of disapproval, disappointment or disgrace. Shame is a painful <u>feeling</u> of humiliation or distress caused by the consciousness of wrong, indignity, and embarrassment. Stigma is a <u>mark</u> of disgrace associated with a particular circumstance, quality or person.

Can you see the progression?

i. **First is an Expression of Reproach**: This is something that someone says, shows, or does to you that expresses disapproval, disappointment or disgrace. This word or action becomes a seed planted by the enemy in your mind that begins the process of emotional trauma. Many times, the actual words spoken or actions taken were not even meant to be harmful, but the devil steps in and deconstructs or misinterprets those words or actions in your mind. Now, the words or actions become loaded with negative meaning or connotation for you and become very hurtful.

ii. **Shame:** You spend time turning those hurtful words over and over in your mind, until the negative connotation crystalizes, and is internalized. Now you see yourself through those words, and that misinformation, and reproach attaches to you personally, and produces shame. In your mind you see yourself as they described you and take on or adopt their negative description as an accurate assessment. This then leads to or compounds existing feelings and consciousness of insecurity, indignity, humiliation, and embarrassment, and you feel ashamed. By this time, what had started out as a comment about an action or situation, has become internalized as a reflection or assessment of your person. The most insidious part of this process is that the harmful effects of those words, depend only on the weight you give them. You can completely disarm and disempower them by denying them of any weight. For example, if someone called you an old maid because you are not married, that hurts only in proportion to the weight that you place on being married. If you don't put any weight on being married, their comments can roll off you like water off a duck's back. But if you place a lot of weight on being married, then their words can cut very deeply like a branding iron, and you think, "Something is wrong with me".

iii. **Stigma:** Reproach and shame if left to linger and simmer in your mind, will ultimately lead to a stigma, a mark, an invisible brand that you carry around with you, and something that scars your very soul. This mark or label mars you in your own mind, and places a limitation on what you can do, and who you can become.

The sad thing is that the expression of reproach that initiated this tragic cycle may be completely untrue. It could be a malicious, ignorant or mischievous comment that is not based in fact. But if you allow it to penetrate your psyche and linger, it could completely destroy your sense of wellbeing.

The book, "Nothing" by Mick Inkpen, is a remarkable story about a little cloth tabby cat. It has been lying on the floor, in the attic, under heavy boxes full of junk, for many, many, years. It has been there for so long that it could remember very little of anything. It had forgotten all about daylight. It had even forgotten its own name. "I wonder who I am?" It thought. It's owners decided to move to a bigger house to make room for a new baby. The movers arrived and saw the cloth tabby cat in the attic. "What have we got here?" One mover asked? "Oh, it's nothing, let the new people get rid of it" the second mover answered, and they left. "Oh, that's my name", thought the little cloth tabby cat, "Nothing, my name is Nothing". It began to call itself "Nothing". Soon, a mouse accosted it and said, "New people always get rid of you", "You can't stay here, not with new people coming." Then along came a fox who asked, "What on earth are you?" "I'm Nothing" said the little cloth tabby cat. The fox sniffed at it, and said disdainfully, "Nothing worth eating, that's for sure", and trotted off. The little cloth tabby cat was devastated. It could not believe that it had been rejected, even by a fox. Finally, a live tabby cat named Toby came along, and helped the cloth tabby cat reunite with its family. It found out who it was. Its name was not Nothing. Its name was "Little Toby". It was loved by its owners and had a purpose. With a needle, thread, and some cloth, it was restored, and when the new baby was born, it was placed in its rightful place, next to the baby.

Here again, we see the progression! The voice of the mover was the voice of reproach. He said, "Oh, it's nothing". The cloth tabby cat internalized those words, and began to call itself nothing. Then, everybody else began to call it nothing, and soon, they started to treat it as nothing!

I see this tragic cycle repeated in the lives of so many Christian singles. Due to wrong words, comments, and actions by friends, colleagues or church members, many Christian singles are made to feel forgotten or on the fringes, both in society, and sadly in their churches. Their self-esteem is compromised and they are emotionally vulnerable. After a couple failed attempts to connect or get a date online, the devil whispers to them, "Something is wrong with you". Then they go to school, and because they are not sleeping around like everybody else, a classmate calls them weird. At church on Sunday, they are bombarded with messages and images about marriage, as if marriage is the only option, and if you are not married, then something is wrong with you. So, the single person feels out of place, invisible, and overlooked even in the church. They are either not invited or decline invitations to go to church events because most of the other attendees are married. Now the devil is really talking to them. Everywhere they go, they are made to feel defective in some way because they are not married.

Unfortunately, in many instances, this negative pressure is reinforced by family members who speak damaging words to the single person, making them feel unattractive, and unwanted. They point to other relatives and friends who are getting married, and ask, "What is wrong with you?" This is a devastating onslaught, and sadly, little by little, the single person begins to believe the lie. Next thing you know, they are thinking, "Something is wrong with me". Then, most damaging of all, they begin to see, talk to, and about themselves as if something is wrong with them. Over time, this does incalculable damage to their self-image, self-definition, and self-esteem. They feel worthless, hopeless, and meaningless. And they begin to project that vibe on to others. This sets them up for predators and manipulators, who would want to take advantage of them, and exploit their vulnerable emotional state.

Meanwhile, none of this is based in truth. None of these negative attitudes, comments or feelings are based in scripture. In fact, the Bible teaches that we must see ourselves through the lens of the word of God, and not the opinions of other people; and that we must say about ourselves only what God says about us, not what we think or what other people say. This is critical because what we believe and say about ourselves has the greatest impact on our lives more than any other person's words spoken over us. God's word empowers every single person to value themselves, celebrate their season of singleness, and live a life filled with God's presence, purpose, passion, and power.

2. Comparison and Competition: We live in a "social media" world. A fake world powered by cell phones, cameras and technology that can make the lives of others look flawless and exceptionally glamorous, and ours look humdrum by comparison. This set up can generate significant discontent, stress, and envy that erodes our peace, and undermines wellness in our souls. I once saw a program on TV where they showed a photo posted on social media. At first blush, it looked like the photo of a beautiful woman in a sexy bathing suit, lounging in a beach chair, with the ocean waves gently lapping at her feet, against the backdrop of majestic palm trees. She looked the perfect picture of glamor, luxury, and sophistication in a tropical paradise. Then they stepped back and offered a wide shot of the camera. I was shocked to see that the beautiful ocean paradise was nothing more than a paper backdrop and the lapping of the ocean waves against her feet was really the motion of water in a small tub. Her feet were soaking in a small foot spa! In reality, this woman was sitting in a beach chair in the back of a rather rundown house, but with the wonders of technology and social media, she was projecting a life of luxury that was completely bogus. What a stark contrast between what was projected and the harsh reality! When I watched that show, I wondered how many people had compared their real lives to the fake lives, and smiles presented on social media, and had envied that woman in the photo, and others like her for their "perfect life"?

Comparison is the act of considering the similarities or dissimilarities between two things or people. Comparison in and of itself is not bad, if it is a factual, sterile, outline and evaluation of reality. The problem is, that it rarely is. It is loaded with emotions, mis-interpretations, and personal judgements that are often woefully inaccurate. As in the story above, we rarely ever know the full reality of another person's life. We only know what we see projected publicly and comparing ourselves to them on that basis is flawed. "It's fairly easy to envy one aspect of another person's life – his/her figure, talent, wealth, significant other or intelligence. It's much harder to examine and then envy a whole life – a complete compendium of experiences" (*Let's Stop Comparing Ourselves, Aabye-Gayle*). Nobody has a perfect life.

The Bible warns against comparing ourselves with others. Second Corinthians 10:12 states, "In measuring themselves against each other and comparing themselves with each other, they are not wise." Most comparison is unhealthy for the soul. This is because comparison has a twin sister named competition, and a partner in crime named envy. They blind us to the many things that God has blessed us with, and focus us on, and amplify, the few things that somebody else has, that we don't have. This is why President

Theodore Roosevelt said that, "Comparison is the thief of joy". "Comparison is corrosive. It eats away at my ability to be content and confident" (*Aabye-Gayle*). Of course, not all comparison is bad. In 1 Corinthians 11:1, Paul said, "Imitate me as I imitate Christ". This is holy imitation. "Holy imitation is not about cramming ourselves into another's mold. It's about recognizing the Christlike principles another has applied to their life and figuring out how to apply them to ours" (*Comparison is not the Thief of Joy, Abigail Dodds*). The key to holy imitation is, "Leading our comparisons in the right direction – away from envy, pride, covetousness, and self-pity, and toward Christlike imitation and the fear of God" (Dodds). This type of imitation or comparison can turn us into better parents, mentors and friends.

3. Strife and Contention: Strife is an unpleasant word, even its sound is unpleasant. It describes conflict, disagreement, argument, bickering, and controversy. Contention is the noise of relational strife. It is the quiet, seething, undercurrent of ongoing friction. Strife and contention are arch enemies of wellness, not only in the soul, but also in the body. Medical science has long linked strife and contention to a long string of ailments including, hypertension, heart disease, obesity, asthma, diabetes, headaches, gastrointestinal problems, and even Alzheimer's disease. (10 Health Problems Related to Stress, R Morgan Griffin). This state of prolonged friction is very damaging to the soul – mind, emotions, relationships, and physical health. It breeds fear, worry, anxiety, and panic attacks. Strife and contention are the direct opposites of peace, are extremely hazardous to health, and are major contributors to an unwell soul and body.

4. Worry and Anxiety: This is when we focus on, and meditate on our problems. Worry, fear, and anxiety is what results when we let the trouble around us get inside our souls. The Bible instructs us to fix our eyes on Jesus, who is the author and finisher of our faith (Hebrews 12:2). Second Corinthians 4:17-18 states, "For our present troubles are small and won't last very long. Yet they produce for us a glory that vastly outweighs them and will last forever! So, we don't look at the troubles we can see now, rather we fix our gaze on things that cannot be seen. For the things we see now will soon be gone, but the things we cannot see will last forever". This is the key to overcome worry and anxiety. Fixing our gaze on God and His awesome power and not on our problems. When we fixate on our problems, we look through the lens of fear, and "The lens of fear magnifies the size of uncertainty" (Chuck Swindoll). Also, worry and anxiety focuses on us and our ability to solve our problems. It fixates on our resources or lack thereof, and searches desperately within our personal resource pool for a means or avenue to meet the need at hand, and when we come up short, as we often do, it hits the panic button in our minds. However, God did not intend that we should live this way. In Matthew 6:25, He tells us not to worry, and in verse 27, He asks rhetorically "Can all your worries add a single moment to your life?" His point is the utter uselessness of worry. The only thing that worry produces are ulcers.

Sometimes, people are confused about the Bible's injunctions against focusing on the problem. They say, "I can't ignore reality". Well, the story of Abraham illustrates how we can elevate our focus and maintain our faith in the face of physical circumstances that contradict the promises of God.

In Genesis 12, God promised Abraham that He will make him a great nation. However, 25 years passed, Abraham got older, Sarah passed the age of childbearing, and they still were childless. Romans 4:19 says of Abraham: "And not being weak in faith, he did not consider his own body, already dead (since he was about a hundred years old), and the deadness of Sarah's womb". The key word here is *consider*. Another word for it, is meditate or focus on. Abraham did not focus on his daunting physical impediments. "He did not waver at the promise of God through unbelief, but was strengthened in faith, giving glory to God, and being fully convinced that what God had promised He was also able to perform." Abraham did not consider his dead body, He fixed his gaze on the immense omnipotence of Almighty God. Chuck Swindoll put it this way, "The size of a challenge should never be measured by what we have to offer. It will never be enough." Abraham knew this and so, instead of focusing on himself, he fixed his gaze on God. To counter worry, he gave glory to God, focused on the character of God, and verbally affirmed his faith that God will keep His promise, and God did. This is the pattern or model for us as well, to overcome worry and anxiety.

5. Guilt and Condemnation: These are the devil's favorite toys. They corrode our identity in Christ, attack our sense of value, and afflict our conscience. In the Bible, the devil is called, "the accuser of the brethren" (Revelation 12:10). He loves to accuse and heap guilt and condemnation on God's people, for what they may or may not have done. The goal of the devil in accusing us is to afflict, blame, and molest. He wants to undermine our confidence in our relationship with God. He wants to focus us on ourselves, our unworthiness, rather than on Christ's perfection, and complete atonement for us. His design is to create enmity between us and God and to alienate us from our rightful place and authority as children of God. He latches onto any issue, misrepresents facts, ascribes the most egregious wrong motives to our actions, and then impeaches our character. Unfortunately, because there is often some grain of truth in what the devil uses against us, we fall for the lie, and desperately try to defend ourselves or feel condemned, and unworthy to approach God or receive the good things that He has for us. This is a strategic attack, because a Christian robbed of his right standing before God in Christ, now stands in his own merit. That is a dangerous place to be, because you are no longer relying on the victory of Christ, but "facing off against the devil on your own merits. As soon as you take your eyes off Christ, you will see your sin and failure. Now the devil has you on his turf! He will accuse, condemn, oppress, torment, and destroy you" (*Godson*).

Our pathway to victory is the cross and the finished works of Jesus Christ. Because of it, we can talk back to the devil. The Bible says that we overcome him by the blood of the Lamb, and the word of our testimony (Revelation 12:11). So, we can and should talk back to the devil. We can say, "Satan, I rebuke you! There is no condemnation for me, because I am in Christ Jesus (Romans 8:1).

Zechariah 3:1 gives us a vivid pre-incarnation illustration of the accuser in action:

> Then the angel showed me Jeshua the high priest standing before the angel of the LORD. The Accuser, Satan, was there at the angel's right hand, making accusations against Jeshua. And the LORD said to Satan, "I, the LORD, reject your accusations, Satan. Yes, the LORD, who has chosen Jerusalem, rebukes you. This man is like

a burning stick that has been snatched from the fire." Jeshua's clothing was filthy as he stood there before the angel. So the angel said to the others standing there, "Take off his filthy clothes." And turning to Jeshua he said, "See, I have taken away your sins, and now I am giving you these fine new clothes." Then I said, "They should also place a clean turban on his head." So they put a clean priestly turban on his head and dressed him in new clothes while the angel of the LORD stood by. Then the angel of the LORD spoke very solemnly to Jeshua and said, "This is what the LORD of Heaven's Armies says: If you follow my ways and carefully serve me, then you will be given authority over my Temple and its courtyards. I will let you walk among these others standing here. "Listen to me, O Jeshua the high priest, and all you other priests. You are symbols of things to come. Soon I am going to bring my servant, the Branch.

In this scripture, we see Jeshua, the high priest being accused by the devil. He was filthy, as we so often are, so the devil had the right to accuse and challenge him, but the Angel of the Lord (The pre-incarnate Christ), spoke up for Jeshua. He rebuked the devil, removed Jeshua's filthy garments and put a priestly garment on him, complete with the turban that declared, "Holiness unto the Lord". He silenced the devil's accusations.

This is exactly what Jesus did for us by His death and resurrection. Like Jeshua, we were guilty as charged, but Jesus took our sins upon Himself on the cross. He who knew no sin, became sin for us, that we might become the righteousness of God in Him (2 Corinthians 5: 21). Jesus canceled the record of the charges against us and took it away by nailing it to the cross. In this way, He disarmed the spiritual rulers and authorities. He shamed them publicly by His victory over them on the cross (Colossians 2:14). Hallelujah to the lamb of God!

CHAPTER 3

HEALTHY

IF YOU WERE ASKED TO SELECT AN H WORD that accurately captures a key step to wholeness, which word would you choose? I looked at a word cloud for the letter H. Honesty and happy stood out above all the other words. This means that they are the H words most commonly used by people, and would likely make the top ten of many people's favorite word list. Would you have selected them? What about words like holiness, halo, heavenly, and humble. Surely, these words describe attributes and virtues that most Christians hold dear, and strive to model daily. Would you have chosen those words? What of handsome, humor, hot, and hero. If you are a beautiful single woman, like myself, you probably like those words because they are attributes that you'll want in your man! And if you are a single guy, you certainly want those words to be used to describe you. So, would you select them? Well, more than a decade of living a successful and prosperous single life has taught me that the one H word that articulates the next indispensable step to wholeness for the Christian single, is the mundane, humdrum, word, healthy! Healthy is indispensable to wholeness.

For starters, healthy encompasses many of the other H words, and for a Christian, it encompasses all those words. A healthy Christ follower is honest, holy, heavenly minded, and humble. Handsome, humor, hot, happy, and hero is in the eye of the beholder, so every Christian man can certainly look handsome; and every Christian man or woman can be hot, happy, have a sense of humor, and be a hero to someone, even if only their kids.

Like "well", healthy is a word that refers to every aspect of a person's being – spiritual, emotional, mental, social, physical, and so on. The World Health Organization (WHO) defines Health as, "A state of complete physical, mental, and social wellbeing" (*Definition of Health, James S Larson,*). More recently, WHO has added spiritual health to their definition. Man is a tripartite being with a spirit, soul, and body (1 Thessalonians 5:23). To be whole, a person has to be healthy in all three dimensions. In other words, there is no wholeness without health - spiritual, emotional, mental, and physical. Health is a critical component of wholeness.

Healthy Spirit

A healthy spirit is one that is indwelt by God's Holy Spirit. First Corinthians 6:17 states that, "The person who is joined to the Lord is one spirit with Him." So, spiritual health begins with a personal relationship with Jesus Christ. When we are joined to the Lord, His Holy Spirit comes to live in us; and the wholeness and perfection that is in God flows into our spirits and makes our spirits whole and perfect. The Bible makes this point vividly when it states in 1 John 4:17 that, "As He (Jesus) is, so are we in this world". In our spirit, we look exactly like Christ because we are joined with Him. His Spirit joins with our spirit to affirm that we are God's children (Romans 8:16).

In today's world, many people claim to be spiritual and almost anything that involves any belief system can pass for "spiritual". But you need more than just a belief system to be spiritual. The belief system in question has to be able to answer the following four fundamental questions:

1. **Origin:** Where did we come from?

2. **Meaning:** Why are we here and what is the purpose of life?

3. **Morality:** How do we develop a moral framework, and make decisions about right or wrong, good or bad?

4. **Destiny:** Where are we headed and how should we live in light of that?

The Christian faith provides a coherent answer to these four questions, and therefore a valid and credible framework for spiritual health.

Spiritual health has grown in significance in recent years. It has been described as, "The need for: meaning, purpose and fulfillment in life; hope, will to live; belief and faith" (*The Spiritual Dimension, Ross L.*). It is widely recognized as important for the overall attainment of health, wellbeing, and quality of life. So, "an individual with high levels of spiritual wellness will experience increased physical, social, and emotional health" (*What is Spiritual Health? Study.com*).

Healthy Soul

A healthy soul is foundational to overall health. Third John 2 states, "Beloved, I pray that you may prosper in all things and be in health, just as your soul prospers." This scripture makes soul prosperity foundational. It shows that physical health and prosperity "in all things" flow from the wellspring of a healthy and prosperous soul.

So, what is a healthy soul? A healthy soul is a soul at rest. It is a soul that is, "not emotionally distraught. It doesn't worry or become anxious, fret, and fear. It is not burdened with guilt and shame. It has found its home in God and trusts Him to take care of all that concerns it" (*Healing the Soul of a Woman, Joyce Meyer*). A healthy soul includes mental and emotional health, as well as freedom from addictions and oppression.

Mental Health: The World Health Organization defines mental health as, "A state of well-being in which every individual realizes his or her own potential, can cope with the normal stresses of life, can work productively and fruitfully, and is able to make a contribution to her or his community" (*Mental health, WHO*).

Another definition of mental health developed by European psychiatrists is, "A dynamic state of internal equilibrium which enables individuals to use their abilities in harmony with universal values of society. Basic cognitive and social skills; ability to recognize, express and modulate one's own emotions, as well as empathize with others; flexibility and ability to cope with adverse life events and function in social roles; and harmonious relationship between body and mind, represent important components of mental health which contribute, in varying degrees to the state of internal equilibrium" (*Mental Health Christopher Lane Ph.D*).

From these definitions, it is clear that mental health is a critical component of and can seriously affect daily life, relationships, and physical health. Mental illness is a disorder that affects the mood, thinking, and behavior. It includes anxiety disorders, mood disorders, schizophrenia, psychotic disorders, dementia, and eating disorders. Sometimes, mental illness is caused by a chemical imbalance in the brain. Also, stress, family problems, and problems at work or school can precipitate mental illness or make it worse.

Emotional Health: Emotional health is a very important part of overall health. "People who are emotionally healthy are in control of their thoughts, feelings, and behaviors. They are able to deal with life's challenges. They can keep problems in perspective and bounce back from setbacks. They feel good about themselves and have good relationships" (*Mental Health, familydoctor.org*). Keep in mind that emotionally healthy people still feel stress, and negative emotions like anger and sadness. But they know how to manage and effectively navigate these feelings.

Emotional health is not about the problems you have, because everyone has problems. It's more about your approach to, and effectiveness in managing your problems. In her article, 7 Signs of Emotional Wellness, psychologist and author, Dr. Shannon Kolakowski, outlines seven tell-tale indicators of emotional health.

1. **You Treat Others Well:** Emotionally healthy people treat others well. Viewing other people with compassion and treating them with kindness is a hallmark of your own emotional wellbeing. Psychologists call this prosociality. It means that you tend to be sensitive to the needs and feelings of other people, and consider it important to help others. Simply stated, emotionally healthy people are others focused.

2. **You Like Who You Are:** Emotionally healthy people like themselves. When you are emotionally

healthy, you generally feel pretty good about your-self. You know who you are – your foibles, quirks, and strengths, and you're okay with who you are. You're also congruent, meaning that the person you show to the outside world is reflective of who you are on the inside. While there are situations where you naturally shift your attitude or behavior a bit depending on the social circumstance, congruence means that your overall sense of who you are feels in line with what you show others.

3. **You Are Flexible and Adaptable:** Emotionally healthy people have the ability to adapt to all kinds of situations that life throws at them. When you are emotionally healthy, you are able to effectively assess your surroundings, your emotions, and oth-er's reactions to a given situation and use these fac-tors to decide the best course of action. You stand up for yourself when you need to, but also let others have the last word. You know how to have tough conversations, and set boundaries, but you also know how to let things go. You approach life and relationships with openness, a sense of curiosity, and willingness to adapt strategy to circumstances.

4. **You Express Gratitude for Your Loved Ones:** Emotionally healthy people feel and show gratitude for the people and things in their lives. They pur-posefully look at life with a sense of appreciation

for what they have, rather than focusing on what they don't have. Research has shown that counting your blessings has strong benefits for emotional well-being. Also, emotional health is enhanced by your ability and willingness to receive social support. This means that you have people in your life that you can depend on, friends and family, who have your best interest at heart. Being emotionally healthy means that in your relationships, you feel safe to express how you feel, and you feel respected, and validated by those closest to you.

5. **You Are in Touch with Your Emotions:** Another sign of emotional health is that you embrace your emotions – sadness, anger, anxiety, joy, fear, excitement—as a natural and normal part of life. You know that its normal to have periods of stress, are able to manage and express yourself when you feel upset, and know who you can go to, to get comfort or help. You handle and acknowledge your difficult emotions without being overwhelmed by them, or denying that they exist. Emotional health comes from being able to identify, recognize, and accept tough emotions, but still move forward from them without getting stuck. Being emotionally healthy means you might get nervous before going on a date, but you don't let that stop you from going.

6. **You Have Meaning in Your Life:** Emotionally healthy people have a sense of meaning and purpose in life. Emotional health includes living beyond yourself and having passion, a mission, a cause, or larger meaning and purpose to your life. This happens when you use your time and resources to help something or someone that you believe in, for example, volunteering at your child's school, or at a religious or community service organization. Being part of something you connect with and care about is largely associated with emotional well-being and longevity.

7. **You Value Experience More Than Possessions:** Emotionally healthy people value people. "People who tend to highly value attaining wealth, popularity or attractiveness tend to be less emotionally well-off, than people who value self-fulfillment and helping others. People with high levels of emotional health tend to spend their money on experiences, rather than material possessions" (*Kolakowski*). Experiences contribute to emotional health because they lead to shared memories and bonding with people, help you enjoy the beauty in the world, and cultivate the positive emotions that come with new experiences.

Based on these signs of emotional health, how would you score yourself? On a scale of 1-10, what is your self-assessment? Are you emotionally healthy?

God Wants You to Have a Healthy Soul

As we learned earlier, the arena of the soul is the theatre of intense conflict and ongoing warfare. The devil targets and bombards the soul with a daily barrage. His goal is to destabilize, disrupt, and discombobulate. His favorite tools include fear, worry, anxiety, depression, suicidal thoughts, hopelessness, rejection, low self-esteem and self-worth, guilt, condemnation, and so on. The devil mounts a constant attack against us in our minds and emotions, his ultimate goal being, to bring pressure on our will to make the wrong choice, in thought, word or action. Wrong choices when repeated, develop a habit, and over time, habits build character and define our destiny.

While there are mental and emotional illnesses driven by chemical imbalance in the brain, many of the devil's nefarious activities and demonic oppression can manifest as mental illness. Several times in the Bible, Jesus identified and unmasked the devil at work, even though he was hidden under the cloak of sickness, infirmity or mental illness. Again, and again, Jesus would identify the evil spirit at work, cast it out, and deliver the person. Examples include the mute man in Luke 11:14; the deaf and mute man in Mark 9:25; Mary Magdalene in Matthew 9:34; the woman with a spirit of infirmity in Luke 13:11; the demoniac in Matthew 8:28-34; and so on. These scriptures illustrate the point that deliverance is a very effective approach to dealing with the types of mental illness driven by demonic activity or traffic. Later in this chapter is a detailed, step-by-step, deliverance prayer outline to help you break free from demonic oppression.

How to Cultivate a Healthy Soul

Benjamin Franklin's axiom that, "An ounce of prevention is worth a pound of cure" is true in mental and emotional health as in other areas of health. The best approach to maintaining a healthy soul is to keep from getting sick in the first place, or to recover and bounce back as quickly as possible after ill health. As in other areas of health, exercise and diet are the critical building blocks of a successful preventative mental and emotional health regimen. Here are some steps for maintaining a healthy soul:

1. **Meditate on God and His Word:** Exercising your mind daily on the truth of the word of God provides required conditioning for a healthy soul. Joshua 1:8 gives us the prescription, "Study this Book of Instruction continually. Meditate on it day and night so you will be sure to obey everything written in it. Only then will you prosper and succeed in all you do." Meditation means to think deeply or focus one's mind for a period of time on something. It means to ponder, reflect, cogitate, and contemplate. It means to turn over and over in the mind like the

cow chews the cud. It also means to mutter or speak the words out repetitively. Meditation on the scripture saturates the mind with the thoughts of God and keeps the mind focused on God. Meditation is a soul tranquilizer. It anchors the soul in God and leads to inner peace.

2. **Praise and Worship:** Praise and worship supplies the essential vitamins for soul health. Colossians 3:16 gives us the prescription, "Let the word of Christ dwell in you richly in all wisdom, teaching and admonishing one another in psalms and hymns and spiritual songs, singing with grace in your hearts to the Lord." The word of God is Jesus himself (John 1:1). So, if you surround yourself with worship that is based on the word of God, there is no room in your mind for the devil to occupy. The word of God is Spirit and life (John 6:63). It will minister the life of God into every aspect of your being and drive away death, bondage, and oppression in all its forms. When you confront, and are squeezed by a stressful situation, whatever is inside you will spill out. If you are full of the word of God, you will respond to your situation with psalms, hymns, and spiritual songs, instead of bitterness, vitriol, anger, and cursing. This is the best medicine for mental health ever! First Samuel 16:14-23 provides a vivid illustration. It describes how Saul, the king of Israel, was tormented by an evil spirit, which manifested in depression, fear, anxiety,

and paranoia, but whenever the tormenting spirit troubled Saul, "David would play the harp. Then Saul would feel better, and the tormenting spirit would go away." Singing psalms, hymns, and spiritual songs will give you a buoyant, healthy, soul free from bondage and oppression!

Take thoughts captive with words. Words can stop a train of thought dead in its tracks.

---

3. **Renew Your Mind:** Renewing your mind is the soul therapy prescribed in Romans 12:2. It simply means exchanging your thoughts for the thoughts of God. The word of God tells you who you are in Christ, what you have in Him, and what you can do through Him (Philippians 4:13). Renewing your mind means that once you find out what the Bible says, you believe it as truth, and if your own thoughts on an issue are different or inconsistent with what the Bible says, you set aside your thoughts, and replace them with what the Bible says. When you do this, the word of God will change you, guaranteed, because, God's thoughts and ways are infinitely higher than human thoughts and ways (Isaiah 55:8-9). So, when we receive God's thoughts, it elevates our thinking and perspective. God's word strengthens you, enables

you to see yourself through the eyes of God, and empowers you to prevail over every devise of the devil.

4. **Take Control of Your Thoughts:** "Who we are is shaped moment by moment by the thoughts we let into our mind and heart." (*Every Thought Captive, Steve Lenk*). So, to have a healthy soul and win the battle of the mind, we must take control of our thoughts. Proverbs 23:7 states that, "as a man thinks in his heart, so is he." In other words, we are the sum total of our thoughts. But how can we control the multitude of thoughts that run through our mind each day? Second Corinthians 10:5 states that we can capture our thoughts and teach them to obey Christ. Another translation says that we can take our thoughts captive. These scriptures make us responsible for our thoughts. This is wildly different from popular belief, that we are powerless to control our thoughts, and that they can fly in and out of our minds at will. As Martin Luther said, "You cannot keep birds from flying over your head but you can keep them from building a nest in your hair." Same thing applies to thoughts. You may not be able to control what thoughts pop into your head, but you can control what thoughts occupy your mind. So, how do you take thoughts captive? With words. Words slice through and stop a train of thought dead in its tracks. It does not allow that thought to complete. So, if you have wrongful

thoughts that pervade your mind, speak the word of God right in the middle of that thought process, and it will interrupt, arrest, and short circuit the thought. Then replace that thought with a different thought from the Bible. Philippians 4:8 gives us a list of thoughts that we can think. It says, "Fix your thoughts on what is true, and honorable, and right, and pure, and lovely, and admirable. Think about what it excellent and worthy of praise".

5. **Deliverance Prayer:** Deliverance from demonic oppression is critical to the condition of the soul. Jesus came to set us free. We must make a choice to live free. Galatians 5:1 declares, "So, Christ has truly set us free. Now make sure that you stay free, and don't get tied up again in bondage." This scripture is clear. We have the responsibility to maintain the freedom that Christ purchased for us. John 8:36 affirms our freedom in Christ, "So if the Son sets you free, you are truly free". Freedom is your birthright as a child of God, but you must guard and enforce that spiritual inheritance! So, if you are entangled in emotional bondage, oppression or substance abuse, you can be free! God has done His part; the next move is yours. All you need to do is to appropriate the finished works of Christ, and enforce your deliverance. A prayer outline to break free from curses and satanic covenants is provided in chapter one, and a prayer outline to break soul ties is pro- vided in chapter five.

Below is a deliverance prayer outline. Apply these steps to dispossess the devil, shut down his demonic operation, cut off demonic traffic from your home, and set yourself and others free from oppressive demonic influences.

How to Pray Deliverance Prayer

1. Declare that you are a child of God, an heir of God and a joint heir with Christ. You are seated in heavenly places in Christ Jesus. You are a partaker of God's divine nature and have the mind of Christ (Galatians 4:7, Ephesians 2:6).

2. Declare that you belong to God, and are bought with the precious blood of Jesus (Ephesians 1:7).

3. Declare that the Bible says in Isaiah 54:14, that you shall be far from oppression, and that it shall not come near you.

4. Declare that you are the righteousness of God in Christ. You do not stand in your own authority, ability or righteousness. You stand in the finished works of Christ alone (2 Corinthians 5:21).

5. Bind the strongman spirit of heaviness, and the strongman spirits of fear, bondage, and infirmity, and cast them out of your life (Matthew

12:29). Loose the Holy Spirit, the comforter, garment of praise, oil of joy, and the Spirit of power, love, and a sound mind

6. Rebuke every spirit of oppression operating in your life. Speak directly to the spirit, for example, if you are dealing with depression, you can say, "You spirit of depression, I rebuke you in the name of Jesus. I bind you and shut down your demonic operation in my life. I terminate your access into my life and mind, and command you to pack up now and vacate my life in the name of Jesus."

7. Cut off every demonic traffic in your mind, life, and home. Renounce, destroy or burn any articles, magazines, objects, tokens, mementos, and so on, that are connected to, support or enforce the bondage or demonic oppression (Acts 19:19). Declare that God has delivered you from the dominion of darkness and transferred you into the kingdom of His dear son, who purchased your freedom and forgave your sins (Colossians 1:13).

8. Declare that you are an ambassador for Christ (2 Corinthians 5:20), and your home is the embassy of the kingdom of heaven. So, nothing defiled or unclean is allowed in your home.

9. Disallow access to every agent of the devil into your life. Declare: "Every person with an assignment from hell to distract, stop or limit me, I reject and remove from my life".

10. Declare, "I close every door that I opened to the devil through wrong thoughts and negative words. I refuse to walk in fear, anxiety, worry, doubt, and unbelief. In Jesus name, I declare that I am delivered from emotional trauma, depression, oppression, and addictions" Amen!

11. Take communion to declare your union with Christ and deliverance from the devil and his kingdom.

6. **Break Personal Vows:** Vows we make to ourselves can bring us into bondage. When a person has had a bad experience, been the victim of injustice, or has been mistreated, a natural response is to try to defend and protect oneself from going through that again. Sometimes we do this by making promises or vows to ourselves; like, "Nobody will ever treat me that way again" or "I will never be poor again". While this is understandable and sounds ok, it really is not. You are making a covenant with yourself that does not include God. It is a covenant energized by the flesh and relying on human ability. Also, it is a heart matter, and the motivation is flawed or

questionable at best. Sometimes personal vows are vengeful. At other times, it is your attempt to take care of and protect yourself, and is really a vote of no confidence in God. You have to take care of yourself, because nobody, including God, is taking care of you. The focus of personal vows is yourself, your resources, ability, and oversight over your life. Personal vows can become blind spots that make people impervious to moral lapses, or they can be used to justify moral compromise, drive ungodly ambition, and lead people to side-step their biblical convictions to keep the vows they made to themselves. A personal vow to "never be poor again" can drive an approach to wealth creation that overlooks biblical values. Also, personal vows can lead to a rebellious attitude to godly authority in our lives, and foster an ungodly independence from any "restraints" including the loving restraints of God and His word. Personal vows are the perfect set-up for a "self-made" man/woman mindset. Simply stated, personal vows can provide a gateway to the devil to gain a foothold in your life.

How to Break Personal Vows

To break personal vows, take the following steps:

1. **Repent:** Talk to the Lord about the situation/experience or circumstance that drove the vow.

SINGLE AND HAPPY

2. **Confess:** Confess the underlying lack of trust in
    God. Lay before Him every lingering resentment
    for allowing you to be mistreated, not answering
    your prayers for help, and so on. Tell God that
    you cannot take care of yourself. You don't even
    know what the next hour will bring. Tell him
    that you trust His working in your life.

3. **Forgive:** Forgive the other person who hurt,
    mis- treated or abused you.

4. **Cancel Every Vow:** Renounce and revoke the
    personal vows. Since they were enacted ver-
    bally, you can undo and cancel them verbally.
    Jesus has set you free, and whom the Son sets
    free is free indeed. Declare that you walk in
    your freedom in Christ.

5. **Bind the Strongman:** Bind the strongman
    spirit of haughtiness, and the strongman spirits
    of jealousy, and fear, and cast them out of your
    life (Matthew 12:29). Loose the Holy Spirit, the
    humble and contrite spirit, the love of God, and
    the Spirit of power, love, and a sound mind

6. **Bind the Demons:** Bind the wicked spirits sent
    by the devil and his strongmen to supervise and
    enforce the personal vow in your life. Terminate

106

their assignment, shut down their operation and cast them out.

7. **Plead the Blood:** Declare that the blood of Jesus purchased your salvation and deliverance, and that the blood is speaking over you, freedom, deliverance, victory, strength, favor and grace.

8. **Take Communion:** Take communion to declare your union with Christ and deliverance from the devil and his kingdom.

Healthy Conscience

A key part of a healthy soul is having a healthy conscience. Our conscience represents the God consciousness in us. It is the inner voice or moral compass that helps us to navigate the questions of right and wrong, and make decisions and choices about what is good or bad. The English Oxford Dictionary defines the conscience as the, "moral sense of right and wrong, viewed as acting as a guide to one's behavior." The conscience has two components; 1) A built-in consciousness of the morality of one's own conduct, intentions or character; and, 2) A feeling of obligation to do right or be good. This is why people get a "guilty conscience" when they do not follow the dictates of their conscience, or have a clear conscience when they do. The Bible says that God has written His moral code in our minds and upon our hearts (Hebrews 10:16). This code is the conscience.

Steve Gallagher, in his article, *"The Searing of the Christian Conscience"*, draws a parallel with the physical body. He writes,

> "In the physical realm, the conscience is comparable to the human nervous system. When a person is wounded, he feels pain – the body's inherent means of alerting him that something is wrong. Likewise, when a person sins, the human soul has a warning system that sounds an alarm because the person's actions have wounded him spiritually. The soul-alarm trumpets, "Mayday! Mayday! Something is wrong! He senses that his actions are not only wrong but will also result in destructive consequences"

Since guilt, condemnation, and other negative emotions can result from the state of our conscience, a healthy conscience is important to emotional health. The Bible speaks a lot about the conscience. First Timothy 1:19 instructs us to hold onto faith and a good conscience, and warns that rejecting either would lead to shipwreck. It gives us examples of people like Hymenaeus and Alexander who violated their consciences, and as a result destroyed their faith. In 1 Timothy 4:2, apostle Paul warns that through repeated sin and disobedience to the promptings of the Holy Spirit, our consciences could become seared as with a branding iron and insensitive.

Gallagher, in his article, describes four types of consciences.

Four Types of Consciences

1. **A Tender Conscience:** A person with a tender conscience is keenly aware of every infraction against the Lord. He recognizes sin for the ugly thing that it is and remains consistently open to the Holy Spirit's conviction. He is not looking to push the limits of sin to see how much he can get away with, but to avoid it altogether. Sin to him is a poison which must be eradicated at all cost (Psalms 139:24).

2. **A Wandering Conscience:** This is when bright and innocent faith is slowly supplanted by cynicism, the world's attractions regain their carnal luster, old idols are re-erected within the heart and once forsaken sins start to resurface. This is the process of inner moral decay that occurs when a person allows sin to re-establish itself within their heart. If the person continues along this course, he will soon lose the sense of the evil nature of sin (1 Timothy 1:5-6, Titus 1:15).

3. **A Seared Conscience:** The person who willfully and habitually gives himself over to sin loses the ability to

feel the spiritual pain of his sin. As his heart becomes increasingly calloused, the spiritual system God constructed within him slowly loses its ability to detect the damage being done to it. If the person remains in sin long enough, he can reach the point where he is no longer influenced by the Holy Spirit. He has become so hardened that he would not listen to and does not want to hear the Holy Spirit. If left unabated, this will eventually lead to the death of the conscience.

4. **A Renewed Conscience:** When a man in habitual sin genuinely repents, acknowledges his guilt and takes steps to put it behind him, his hardened heart begins to soften, and he gradually begins to feel the conviction of the Holy Spirit once again. The Bible describes this process as God removing "the heart of stone" and replacing it with "a heart of flesh" (Ezekiel 36:26). Finally, this person is back in the place where God can reach him and help him overcome.

The human conscience truly is a gift from God, to help us to maintain a soft heart, a healthy soul, and an ear that is attuned to the voice of the Holy Spirit.

Healthy Body

God Made Your Body: The human body is an amazing and beautiful work of art made by our great and awesome God. It is also a very complex machine made up of many different types of cells that together create a dizzying array of tissue and organ systems. These include the skeletal, cardiovascular, nervous, digestive, lymphatic, respiratory, reproductive, endocrine, urinary, muscular, and integumentary systems. These systems are populated by a multitude of organs that work synchronously, and in close coordination to seamlessly execute the highly complex daily operations of all human bodily functions.

Do you know that the human femur can support a weight thirty times that of the human body, making it even stronger than steel? Do you know that the human nervous system can relay electrochemical messages at a rate of 249 mph (400 km/hr)? (*Encyclopedia Britannica*). Do you know that, "The human eye contains more than two million operational parts that process up to 35,000 bits of information every hour? It is one of the most complex organs in the body, second only to the brain" (*Key -Whitman Eye Center*).

The body is absolutely amazing! Which is why it is ludicrous for anyone to contend that the human body, with all these amazing feats and features developed randomly by accident. The level of precision required in the functions of the body, the mammoth organization that it entails for the systems of the body to complete all these functions in close coordination, and the fact that most of these functions are routinely repeated over and over each day, belies that claim. The Bible is clear, we were made by God. Psalm 139:13-15 proclaims this truth, "You made all the delicate, inner parts of my body and knit me together in my mother's womb. Thank you for making me so wonderfully complex! Your workmanship is marvelous – how well I know it."

Steward Your Body

Your body is the packaging that houses your spirit and soul. It also houses the five senses that enable you to connect with and function in the earth realm. You cannot fulfill God's plan for your life and for the earth without a body. Simply stated, we need our bodies or "earth suits" to function on this planet because only beings with or in a body have authority in the earth. Therefore, the state of your bodily wellbeing will determine your ability to execute God's plans and purposes for your life. Given the import of the body, it is little wonder how much time and attention the devil devotes to ensure that we neglect, abuse or destroy our bodies.

The health of your body is so important that Jesus paid dearly for it. Isaiah 53:5 and 1 Peter 2:24 says, that by the horrendous stripes that tore His back to shreds, you were, and are healed. So, Jesus fully paid for your health on the cross, but God didn't stop there. Your health is so important that God made your body to heal and repair itself. With the right foods, drinks, rest, and other inputs, your body will heal and regenerate itself. And when an intruder comes in the form of sickness, it will dispatch its police force, the lymphatic system, to go to battle and intercept, stop, arrest, and eject the intruder.

God has done His part in taking care of our bodies. But as in most things, it is a partnership. We as caretakers or stewards of our bodies, have to do our part to ensure our bodily health and wellbeing.

Physical Health and Fitness

It is hard to over-emphasize the importance of physical health and fitness. An unhealthy body can severely hamper our ability to serve God and build His kingdom, or contribute meaningfully to society. Further, it could stop us from being able to fulfill our God-given assignments to love and care for our families. It is therefore of crucial importance that we invest in our physical health and wellbeing. There are individuals who have medical or other conditions that impose physical exercise limits. However, for many of us who are not medically or otherwise constrained, we need to take action daily to contribute to our physical fitness. As stated earlier, God has already done His part in providing for our health. Staying fit is our responsibility. It involves daily exercise and healthy eating habits. My challenge to you is to invest in your physical health. Make moves, not excuses. Here's how.

Make moves, not excuses.

Five Components of Fitness: There are five components used to measure fitness in health clubs and fitness facilities. Tyler Read describes them in his article, *"Top 5 Health-Related Components of Fitness"*.

1. **Cardiovascular Endurance:** Also known as cardio-respiratory endurance, this measures the capacity at which blood and oxygen is delivered throughout the body to fuel continuous activity. The delivery of oxygen and nutrients begins all of our bodily processes, which makes cardiovascular endurance the most important of all the health and fitness components. A weak cardiovascular system can lead to multiple health problems, including heart attack and stroke. To improve cardiovascular endurance, you need to exercise at a sufficient level of intensity to elevate your heart rate. Your heart is a muscle and like all muscles, need exercise to get stronger. Cardio exercises like running, walking, biking, climbing the stairs, and so forth, can help improve cardiovascular endurance.

2. **Muscular Strength:** Muscular strength refers to the ability of your muscles to produce force. When your muscles contract, they produce force to overcome any opposing force. But as the opposing force increases, there comes a point where your muscular contraction cannot produce enough force to overcome it. Increasing the amount of opposing force

your muscles can overcome requires developing your muscular strength. You can do this through resistance training with free weights, elastic bands, body pump workouts, and exercise machines.

3. **Muscular Endurance:** Muscular endurance is a combination of both muscular strength and cardiovascular endurance. It is a measure of how long a muscle can overcome a force before it becomes fatigued. Whereas muscular strength refers to maximal strength, muscular endurance refers to how long the muscles can contract under a light load. To test your muscular endurance, pick up three pound weights and see how many times you can press them over your head before you cannot lift your arms up any longer. To improve your muscular endurance, you can engage in cardiovascular exercises such as walking up a flight of stairs, running, or riding a bike. You can also increase muscular endurance by eating a diet rich in grains. Grains are an excellent source of fuel associated with heightened muscular endurance.

4. **Flexibility:** Flexibility or the range of motion at your joints, is an important aspect of health and injury prevention. A few factors play a role in your flexibility, including how tight or relaxed your muscles are and the mechanics of your joints. Flexibility training comes in many different forms, with static

stretching being the most common. To perform a static stretch, you need to extend the muscle to its most elongated state and hold it there for a time. Daily stretches help to maintain flexibility. Also, vitamins and minerals from natural sources support and maintain flexibility.

5. **Body Composition:** The majority of your body is made up of muscle tissue, fat, and bone. For healthy body composition, the most significant variable is your body fat percentage, or how much of your total body mass is composed of fat tissue. A high percentage of body fat is associated with multiple health problems, including bad cholesterol, high blood pressure, and diabetes. To improve your body composition, reduce your intake of sugar and fat. This combination has long been known to be the cause of surplus body fat.

Rest

A critical component of, and prerequisite for physical health and fitness is rest. Rest is the body's preventative medicine, and one of the most effective protections against sickness, injury, and disease. You think clearer, sleep better and feel more energized when you take time to rest. In today's world, being busy and overscheduled is the norm. "But living in a constant state of crazy-busy with overscheduled to-do lists have a profoundly negative effect on your health" (*Stillness and Rest, Dr. Deborah Anderson*).

God cares more about your
"WHO" than your "DO".

Most people do not plan any downtime, rest, still-ness, or relaxation into their schedules. However, our bodies were not created for endless activity and non-stop engagement. We need time to slow down, check out, unplug, and unwind. Medical science has demon-strated that adequate amounts of rest and sleep pro-mote physical and emotional health, reduce the risk of accidents at home, work, or on the road, and support memory, brain activity, and effective decision making. God created our bodies to need rest, and He estab-lished a pattern of rest for us to emulate. He worked for six days and rested on the seventh day, not because He was tired, but to provide a model for us. He then mandated a sabbath rest as one of the ten command-ments. Jesus replicated this model. Again, and again, He would take time off to rest and recharge (Mark 6:30-31, Matthew 14:23, Luke 6:12).

I heard the story of a pastor who never went on vaca-tion. He was always working and serving his congrega-tion and community. Needless to say, he was burned out. The advisory board of his church pressed him to take time off and recuperate. But he was adamant. His response? "The devil works overtime, he never takes a day off, and neither will I". Well, during prayer, the Lord rebuked him and asked him why he was using the devil as his example? God cares more about our "who" than our "do". This is why He wants us to rest. When you take time to rest, you acknowledge your dependence on God. Rest is your declaration that God is God and you are not. He runs the world and not you. Rest is your reckoning time to check in with yourself and ensure that you are aligned with the things and people that matter in your life. It is your humbling admission that you are a finite resource, in need of refurbishment and sustenance. Do yourself a favor and take a rest!

Body and Self-Image

As a Christian single, you must not let the world cast you into its mold. Hollywood's definition of beauty is a size two woman. That is a lie. God made beautiful women in all shapes and sizes. I personally cannot understand how a grown woman can be a size zero. My immediate question is "Where are you?" I also wonder whether size zero is healthy overall and adequately supports the normal functions of a woman's body. The tragic tales of young women starving themselves and looking like a bag of bones to achieve this dubious standard is heart breaking. Not to mention the eating disorders and other dysfunction that it has engendered.

A Christian woman's focus should be on honoring God in and with her body. She must be a good steward of her body, not so that she can meet Hollywood's standard of beauty, but so that she can be a good caretaker of herself and maintain a healthy body, ready and fit for the master's use. So, as Christians the reason why we exercise and take care of our bodies is because it is the temple of the Holy Spirit, and failure to care for the body will give the devil an inroad to shorten or terminate our ability to serve God on this earth. However, as apostle Paul notes in 1 Timothy 4:8, compared to godliness, physical exercise profits only little. "For bodily exercise profits a little, but godliness is profitable for all things, having promise of the life that now is and of that which is to come." So, do not sacrifice godliness for physical fitness.

To be clear, I strongly encourage everyone to exercise regularly. I have a personal commitment to regular exercise myself. But as with everything in our walk with God, the motive is of utmost importance. I like to look good and I know that working out helps me to look good. But that is not the primary reason why I exercise. I exercise because it helps me stay fit, and take care of my body so I can be a better Christian, woman, mom, friend, sister, and minister of the gospel.

If You don't like what you see in the mirror, change it, because you can!

There are some people who will never be a size six, even if they starved themselves. So, the size is not the issue, being healthy is. Whatever is the healthy size for you, press on to get there and stay there. Be the best you that you can be. Compete only with yourself, to become a better version of you. Accept yourself and love yourself. Let that be your motivation. I work out at the YMCA. In the women's bathroom is a plaque that reads "I work out because I love my body – not because I hate it". That is the right attitude. Love your body enough to take care of it, after all, Jesus paid dearly for you to have a healthy body. Love God and His call on your life enough to take care of your body, so that you don't abort His plan for your life through untimely death or preventable disease. Love your children, family, and friends enough to take care of your body so you are not a burden to them or bring them sorrow, anxiety, and worry through your sickness. Make peace with your thighs and be confident in who you are! If you don't like what you see in the mirror, change it, because you can!

Same thing with the guys. Having a six pack is way overrated. Having a one pack, a heart of gold, and a life that honors God is way more important. If the truth be told, some images of body builders with bulging muscles and ribbed veins can be somewhat frightening. So, you don't have to look like a body builder. All you need is regular exercise to ensure that you run your life's race to the end and finish well. The Bible says of men like Abraham (Genesis 25:8); Moses (Deuteronomy 34:7); and David (1 Chronicles 29:28), that they died at "a good old age." God promises us long life. In Psalm 91:16 He says, "With long life will I satisfy you and show you my salvation." So, we have His promise of longevity, but whether we live long, how we live, and our quality of life depends a great deal on the choices we make to be good stewards of our bodies. I want to die at a good old age, healthy and strong. What about you?

Looking Good

God wants us to look good! He is a royal God. He created beauty and delights in it. He dresses the flowers daily with resplendent splendor and exotic fragrances. He wants His children to represent his grandeur. He wants us to look good. In Exodus, when He gave the specifications for the attire of the priests, He did not skimp or cut corners. It was regal, elegant, and incorporated a lot of gold, and precious jewels. In his home in heaven, the streets are paved with gold, and precious stones lavishly adorn his dwelling place. God is a great king, and He rules in pomp and opulence. He surely wants us, His children, to look good, however, we must look good within the confines of His holiness.

God's holiness is an inward beauty, the precious work of the Holy Spirit within the heart. However, it manifests in the physical and is visible in how we dress, talk, what we do, where we go, the friends we keep, and so on. God's holiness calls us to modesty, in word, deed, and dress. This does not mean wearing no makeup, ankle length dresses, and so on. That is a misinterpretation of holiness. You can dress like that, but not because God's holiness requires it.

With the prolific use of social media and selfies, many Christian women have forgotten the biblical injunction to dress modestly. They flaunt their scantily clad bodies in selfies posted on Instagram, Facebook and other social medial portals. For them the biblical phrase, "Lo and behold" has been wrongly translated to mean low cut blouses that expose their body for all to behold. This type of behavior does not reflect the holiness of God. So, while it is true that ankle length dresses and head covering do not express God's holiness, it is equally true that wearing gaudy clothes that are immodest do not represent the holiness of God (1 Peter 3:3-4).

Healthy Attitude

A healthy attitude is one of the best gifts a person can give themselves. This truth is reflected in the popular saying that, "Your attitude determines your altitude". A healthy attitude is a positive approach to life that makes us more engaged, creative, motivated, energetic, resilient, and productive. It is a positive frame of mind, way of thinking, orientation, and outlook on life. "It's oriented towards finding the best solution(s) to any problems and optimizing your abilities, instead of doing the opposite. And it takes into account others' well-being" *(What is Healthy Attitude? Aparna Muktibodh, Quora).* A healthy attitude and thought process does not mean "playing ostrich", and ignoring the realistic facts of life, on the contrary, a person with a healthy attitude focuses on the facts, but incorporates hope and faith into their thinking about the facts. It means that you understand and acknowledge the facts, but are not overwhelmed, immobilized or paralyzed by them. Rather, you use that information as fuel to energize and help you explore solution options. A healthy attitude is a critical part of effective stress management, which in turn is very important to overall health.

Chuck Swindoll captured the colossal importance of attitude to overall wellbeing when he said, "The longer I live, the more I realize the impact of attitude on life. Attitude, to me, is more important than facts. It is more important than the past, than education, than money, than circumstances, than failures, than successes, than what other people think or say or do. It is more important that appearance, giftedness or skill. It will make or break a company...a church... a home. The remarkable thing is, we have a choice every day regarding the attitude we will embrace for that day. We cannot change our past... we cannot change the fact that people will act in a certain way. We cannot change the inevitable. The only thing we can do is to play on the one string we have, and that is our attitude. I am convinced that life is 10% what happens to me and 90% of how I react to it. And it is the same with you... we are in charge of our attitudes" (*Chuck Swindoll, The Great Awakening*).

Dr. Alan Zimmerman agrees. In his blog, *How to Keep a Positive Attitude When You Don't Feel Like It,* he said, "There simply is no substitute for a positive attitude. It keeps you going when others quit. It releases an abundance of energy....an energy you don't even know you have...and gets you through the toughest times". The blog then quotes General Douglas MacArthur who at 76 years of age, said, "You are as young as your faith, as old as your doubt; as young as your confidence, as old as your fear; as young as your hope, as old as your despair. In the central place of every heart, there is a recording chamber; so long as it receives messages of beauty, hope, cheer and courage; so long as you are young. When the wires are all down and your heart is covered with snows of pessimism and the ice of cynicism, then and only then are you grown old".

Your future is as bright as the promises of God.

A healthy attitude will keep you young, vibrant, hopeful, and full of life, regardless of your age, circumstances, social or economic status. A healthy attitude is foundational to overall health.

How to Develop A Healthy Attitude

1. **Have Faith in God:** Faith is placing complete trust and confidence in someone or something. Placing your faith in God is the most stable, sure and enduring foundation for a healthy attitude. It is believing in the best future that God has for you. God loves you. He created you and has a great plan for your life (Jeremiah 29:11). God believes in you and He empowers you to believe in yourself. He is good and has the blueprint for your future. So, having faith in God and His precious promises will keep your outlook positive, and your future as bright as the promises of God.

---

*Choose your thoughts carefully,
because when you choose your thoughts,
you choose your attitude.*

---

2. **Guard Your Mind:** Your mind has a lot to do with your attitude. If you have a sour, negative, and grumpy attitude, it is more than likely that you have been thinking sour, negative, and grumpy thoughts. So, choose your thoughts carefully, because when you choose your thoughts, you choose your attitude. This is why the Bible tells us what thoughts to populate our minds with. To have a healthy attitude, fill

your mind with thoughts that are true, noble, right, pure, lovely, and honorable (Philippians 4:8).

3. **Be Grateful:** Gratitude is a personal decision to call to mind the good people and things that grace and bless your life; and to take action to recognize and express your appreciation to and for them. It is an act of the will, so you can choose to be and act grateful, even when you don't feel grateful. Being grateful is to remember, memorialize, and treasure the people, things and relationships that give our lives meaning. Gratitude can bring a smile to your face, laughter to your mouth or a tear to your eye, but the posture of the heart is the same – simply and deeply thankful. Often during or at the end of a particularly grueling day, when I am tired and tempted to be downcast, I say to God, under my breath, over, and over again, "I am tired but thankful." This helps me stay focused on the positive and maintain a good attitude. Gratitude enriches your life, as well as the lives of others, and gives you a fresh wind for the next sail. A healthy attitude is an attitude of gratitude, and an attitude of gratitude leads to wholeness. Luke 17:11-19 tells the story of ten men whom Jesus healed of leprosy, but only one of them came back to say, "Thank you". Jesus said to him, "Your faith has made you whole". The other nine lepers were healed, but only this man was healed and made whole because he showed gratitude.

4. **Do the Next Thing**: Having a healthy daily routine is a great boost to a healthy attitude. It provides the personal discipline that helps you to keep going and not wallow in the ditch of self-pity or despair when life hits you hard. A healthy daily routine gives structure to your life and enables you to make good decisions when you are emotionally vulnerable. This is because the good decisions were already pre-made and loaded into your daily or weekly routine. So, all you need to do to get through a tough day, with a good attitude, is to "Do the next thing".

5. **Don't Set Unrealistic Goals:** There are few things as damaging to a healthy attitude as setting unrealistic goals. It leads to disappointment, disillusionment, and discouragement. Goal setting is great, but setting unrealistic goals or expectations is a set up for a big crash, followed by resentment, self-pity, and a host of other negative emotions and attitudes. To cultivate and maintain a healthy attitude, set realistic goals.

6. **Self-Talk:** Self-talk is the endless stream of unspoken thoughts that run through your head. If these thoughts are mostly negative, then your outlook on life is likely to be pessimistic, and vice versa. "Winners say *I can*. That confidence comes from a deeper I AM. For a believer, that confidence comes from knowing who I am and whose I am. I belong to

God. I am a son or daughter of Almighty God. I am seated in heavenly places in Christ Jesus. All things are possible to me because I believe. I *am* so I *can*. Philippians 4:13 (AMP) states, "I can do all things through Him who strengthens *and* empowers me. I am self-sufficient in Christ's sufficiency; I am ready for anything and equal to anything through Him who infuses me with inner strength and confident peace." This verse is the winners creed, and it begins with I *can*. Conversely, losers say: *I don't think I can.* That lack of confidence, hesitation, and self-doubt comes from a deeper *I don't think I am"* (Godson). Positive self-talk promotes a healthy attitude.

> *God believes in you and He empowers you to believe in yourself.*

7. **Celebrate Yourself and Others:** Taking the time to celebrate yourself and others cultivates and supports a healthy attitude. To celebrate yourself is to rejoice and be thankful for your accomplishments, even the "little" ones. You don't have to wait for the grand finale to celebrate. You can have "bite-size" celebrations along the way. When I am doing a big project or have a busy day with a long list of to dos, one of the ways I keep a good attitude is to stop in the middle of the work, survey what we have already

accomplished and say aloud to myself and whoever is working with me, "Little by little, we are getting done!" This declaration tends to boost our energy and keep us motivated. My daughter looks forward to these little celebrations. When we are working together and I pause, look up and smile, she knows what is coming, and she joins me in the joyful celebration of our interim, incremental accomplishments. Together we say with gusto, "Little by little, we are getting done!" This is exactly what God did when He created the world. Genesis 1 gives us the account of creation. It states that God would periodically pause, survey everything that He has already created and say aloud that, "It was good". I encourage you to do the same thing. Celebrate your "little" accomplishments. The Bible tells us to rejoice with those who rejoice. A great way to do that, is to celebrate them and their incremental accomplishments, whether it is a child, spouse, co-worker or friend, this would greatly encourage them to stay the course and finish well.

8. **Make Your Own Sunshine:** If you do, you'll never have another "rainy day". How do you make your own sunshine? By counting your blessings and remembering that you have so much to be thankful for. One of my most frequent prayers under my breath is, "Thank you Lord". On days when I am sensing the beginnings of sadness, or when something happens

that threatens to warp my focus and narrow my vision to the few things in life that I don't have, I remember and begin to verbally thank God, under my breath for seemingly little things, like the fact that I woke up this morning, with a good head on my shoulders. I thank Him for indoor plumbing, a hot shower, for the food on my table, money in my pocket, the blessing of family and friends, the fact that I can drive, that my eyes can see the beautiful world He created, and so on. Every time I go to the store, I leave with a grateful heart, thanking the Lord that I am able to purchase what we need without worrying about how to pay for it. I rejoice in His lavish provision for all our needs. Without fail, my spirit is lifted and I think, "God sees me right now, He knows exactly where I am, I may not have a plan, but He does." Apostle Paul was a super model of this principle. While in jail, he wrote the letter to the Philippians. These are some of the most uplifting and joyful verses in the entire bible. He booms, "Rejoice in the Lord always, and again I say rejoice!" Unbelievable! This is a guy incarcerated in an underground dungeon, probably with open sewer running close by. But that did not stop him because he makes his own sunshine. You can too!

9. **Take Personal Responsibility for Your Life:** Taking personal responsibility for your life is empowering and is indispensable to a healthy attitude. Your

motto should be, "See it, own it, solve it, and do it". This takes away your excuses. It says to you, "It may not be your fault, but it is your responsibility and you can fix it". It activates the I CAN in you. Conversely, whenever you blame someone else, you abdicate responsibility for your life and become powerless to change your situation. If it is somebody else's fault, then you are powerless to fix it. But when you take personal responsibility, you reclaim your power and are able to bring about needed change. A healthy attitude which takes personal responsibility puts you in charge and empowers you to win.

Make your own sunshine and you'll never have another "rainy day!"

10. **Value People:** A fundamental prerequisite to a healthy attitude is valuing people, starting with yourself. It is recognizing that you are a person of tremendous worth and value, and identifying, growing, and owning your personal value. Valuing yourself promotes a healthy attitude, because it helps to balance your perspective, makes you resilient, and enables you to believe in yourself to overcome life's obstacles.

11. See Failure and Setback as an Opportunity:

Failure, setback, and hardship are some of the best teachers in the world. They keep us humble, empathetic, and teachable. A healthy attitude sees failure as an opportunity to grow, learn, become better, and excel. So many times in my life, a situation that I thought was the worst thing to ever happen, eventually turns out to be a blessing in disguise. The Poem, "Along the Road" by Robert Browning Hamilton captures the essence of the value of failure and setback in our lives. He writes:

> I walked a mile with Pleasure
> She chatted all the way,
> But left me none the wiser
> For all she had to say.
>
> I walked a mile with Sorrow
> And ne're a word said she;
> But oh, the things I learned from her
> When Sorrow walked with me!

CHAPTER 4
ON-FIRE

A non-negotiable step to wholeness is a passionate love for Jesus. Whole singles are ablaze with a passionate, committed love for Christ, and a burning desire to help people. First Corinthians 7:34 states that a single person should be, "Devoted to the Lord and holy in body and in spirit". Simply stated, a single person can and should be on-fire for God! We should have hearts, passions, and appetites that are singularly focused, red-hot, tuned in, and fully devoted to God. Christian singles should never feel uncommitted. We should always feel committed in our Relationship to Jesus Christ.

The dictionary defines "on-fire" as, ablaze, fiery, ardent, passionate, fervent, intense, and excited. The Urban Dictionary defines it as, "A term that people use when someone is doing great and they are unable to be stopped." In other words, to be "on fire" is to be fully energized, actively engaged, keenly aware, unstoppable, and living life on full throttle with all cylinders firing. What a sharp contrast to the way many singles live today – merely existing, disengaged, listless, with no joy, excitement, expectancy or fervency. Many singles have checked out on life and are merely going through the motions, simply surviving, putting their lives on hold, and waiting to meet that special someone, before they can start living life to the full. Some single women are coasting through life on auto pilot, desperately hoping to be rescued by a knight in shining armor. Unfortunately, knight in shining armor is the stuff of fairytales.

Passion, zeal, and zest for life is a critical component of wholeness. In other words, there is no wholeness without ardor, fervor, and gusto - spiritually, emotionally, and physically. It is this zeal, enthusiasm, and anticipation that gets you out of bed each morning with a bounce. It is this confluence of passion, zeal, and fire that fuels purpose, invigorates hope, drives expectancy, and a positive outlook on life. All God's children have a tremendous capacity for passion and fire, singles especially.

Where Did the Fire Go?

The lives of single Christians are often marked by apathy and indifference. Some of the indifference is fueled by repeated disappointment and disillusionment. Many have endured prolonged hoping, praying, and believing for a spouse, only to be disappointed, again and again. Over time, the pain of repeated disappointment becomes too much to bear and singles settle for a life of apathy and indifference. Others have been through the devastating trauma of losing a spouse through death or divorce. Life hasn't turned out the way they planned, the dream has become a nightmare, and they are disillusioned.

Many singles are living with a continual, ongoing, low-grade grief that is barely beneath the surface. They are mourning dead marriages, relationships, expectations, dreams, hopes, and goals for the future. Some are mourning the children that they longed for, and had planned to have, but never did, because they never got married. Others are mourning the death of their vision of the future; and yet others are mourning the gap between where they are, and where they had hoped, prayed, believed, and expected to be at this time in their lives. Over time, years of hoping and waiting, with nothing to show for it, takes a toll, and singles lay down their expectancy. They lay down their dreams and desires for the future - a relationship, marriage, home, children, and so on. The harsh reality sets in, the fire goes out, and only the pain remains. Proverbs 13:12 says it well, "Hope deferred makes the heart sick".

The lives of so many singles is like a cemetery, with so much unfulfilled potential. This is why some single people can go from a happy smile and laughter to deep painful sobs in a matter of minutes. Hidden beneath the smiles and pretty makeup is latent grief, pain, and tears over buried dreams. As soon as you breach the cemetery, the grief erupts and spills out through their eyes. So many single Christian women have laid down their desire and expectancy to be mothers, because it's too late now, their biological clock has run out and they can't have children anymore. It's like something inside them, that passionate desire to be a mom, dies and is buried, and they move forward, with a dispassionate, unattached outlook on life. They have smiles on their faces, but their hearts are heavy. For some, they have wept so much that they have no more tears. They don't understand why they are still single, and have tried their best to change it without success. They ask why, and the answers they get back from society, family and friends are demoralizing and they struggle with low self-esteem. Eventually, they make peace with their single status, come to terms with the fact that they may never get married, adjust their expectations, douse their fire, and live detached.

Many single women are eager to get married. As time passes, they come under tremendous pressure to compromise on the word of God, lower their standards, ignore red flags and enter or remain in unsustainable or even ungodly relationships. Sometimes, the guys in question are not born again Christians, at other times, they are "Christians" with very different values and worldviews. Even worse, some women enter, excuse, or remain in the dangerous world of verbal, emotional, physical or sexual abuse, because of fear, low self-worth or lack of financial independence. These women are continually bombarded by negative images and messages. As a result, they have the wrong self-definition and identity, discount themselves, and settle for "whatever they can get".

Single Christian men manage their relational disappointments differently, not with sobs, but with silent screams and coping mechanisms. Prolonged singleness leaves them feeling disconnected, awkward, and incomplete. They want relationships, but are not exactly sure how to make it happen. Prior failures challenge their confidence. So, some settle for the status quo, and tell themselves the lie that they, "don't need anyone". Others go for short term trysts, or the elusive thrill of pornography, while others become devious, self-centered, skilled exploiters of women. This last group troll dating websites with fake personas. They "talk the talk" and know enough "Christianese" to lure single Christian women, but have no genuine commitment to God or His word.

Because many men associate fire, excitement and passion with sex, they typically invest their time, energy, and resources in pursuit of sex and its close relatives. They think that to be "on fire" is to feed their flesh and fulfill their sexual desires. However, the Bible teaches abstinence, so for single Christian men this presents a dilemma. To feed their flesh, they have to ignore the express word of God, override the promptings of the Holy Spirit and justify their sin by claiming that "everyone is doing it." In this lusty morass, their flesh rules and the Spirit is subdued. The more they are "on fire" sexually, the more they feel disconnected from the holy fire of God's presence, which is really what their hearts long for and need. The sexual gratification leaves them feeling empty, guilty, and condemned. What is more, they are not satiated, no matter how much they indulge. Each escapade leaves them more unfulfilled than the last. So, they engage in more and more risky sexual behavior in search of some elusive "fire" or "high". Before long, they are hooked and in bondage to their sensual desires. They are ashamed of their weakness, have little respect for themselves, and are drowning in their secrets. Their willful sin does untold damage to their conscience, identity, and authority as a son of God. Their fleshly lusts rage against the spirit, their spiritual fire goes out, and they live in the "repeat offender" cycle of rebellion, where they willfully disobey the word of God on a routine basis, and do not live a life that pleases God.

Thank God that this is not the story of all single Christian men. There are many who are ardently focused on pleasing God and being sexually pure. But like the women, they too have to grapple with friends, co-workers, and family members who constantly pressure them about being single, make fun of them for having "no game" and encourage them to engage in sexual pursuits. One man was so fed up with being asked, "Are you still single?" that he began to respond, "Are you still married?" It takes a lot of courage, conviction, discipline, and personal commitment for these men of God to stand resolute on the principles of the word of God. I honor and applaud them!

Unfortunately, they also have to contend with deluded "Christian" women, who throw themselves at these men and dangle sex on the one hand and the bible on the other. In this unfortunate scenario, single Christian men feel besieged and think that they are in a no-win situation, and for many, they have no support system within their churches, no accountability partners or network of other strong, committed single Christian men to rely on. Some give in to the pressure, and begin the gradual descent down the slippery slope of the "repeat offender" cycle. Others attempt to assuage their guilt by becoming "engaged" because they think that a perennial engagement will justify or excuse their sexual sin. Either way, their fire dies out and they lie dormant like a volcano.

Dying Embers

When the fire goes out, embers remain. Embers are the glowing coal or wood in a dying fire. It is live and smoldering, but not ablaze. It is hot enough to scald you, but not enough to keep you warm. It has no more flames and is surrounded by ashes. Dying embers can keep water lukewarm, but not hot. It cannot heat up a house, cook food, or crackle. With more wood, fuel, accelerant, and oxygen, it can be fanned back into a roaring fire. But if left untended, it will die out completely, leaving nothing in its wake but ashes.

Unfortunately, this is the emotional and spiritual address where many single Christians live, among the ashes. They are surrounded by ashes of dead and dying relationships, hopes, and expectations. They love God and are committed to living for Him. They go to church regularly and serve in various capacities. They are hot, but not on fire. They believe the promises of God, but would not go out on a limb in faith. "What if God doesn't come through?" They think. They know the Bible is true, but are not sure it will work for their particular situation. They believe God can do all things, but are not sure He will do it for them. They know God answers prayers, but they have unanswered prayers of their own which keeps a lid on their fire, and keeps them from bursting into flames. In one word, many single Christians are lukewarm. This grieves the heart of God, who wants His people, all His people, to be on-fire. He does not want haphazard and half-hearted devotion. He is a passionate and zealous God, and created us with tremendous capacity for passion, drive, and zeal.

God cannot stand lukewarm commitments, expressions, or manifestations. In Revelation 3:15-16, He sharply rebuked the church in Laodicea for being "neither hot nor cold." Then He made a most remarkable statement. He said "I wish that you were either cold or hot. So then, because you are lukewarm and neither cold nor hot, I will spit you out of my mouth." This scripture is amazing. It is saying that God will much rather have a person who is cold spiritually, before He will choose a lukewarm Christian. He would much rather have a person who does not know or profess Christ, than a person who professes faith in Christ, but lacks any fire, passion, and zeal. The first person He will welcome and love, the second person He will abhor, and spit out of His mouth.

This is so different from the way our society has conjured up things. We have been made to believe that, "a little bit of Jesus" is better than none. If we just add a little bit of Jesus to our lifestyle, speech, hobbies, relationships, pre-occupations, and week, then we are good to go. How utterly wrong! Jesus will be Lord of all, or not Lord at all. He says, "You must not have any other god but me" (Exodus 20:3). And in Isaiah 42:8 He states, "My glory I will not give to another". God requires all Christians to be on fire, and singles especially so.

God's Holiness

In Isaiah 6, we see a glimpse of how holy our God is. Isaiah saw a vision of God sitting on His throne, surrounded by His court. Attending Him were mighty Seraphim, each having six wings. With two wings they covered their faces, with two they covered their feet, and with two they flew. They were constantly calling out to each other, "Holy, holy, holy is the Lord of Heaven's armies! The whole earth is filled with His glory!" (Isaiah 6:1-3).

The cry of the Seraphim is not a scripted cry. It is an exclamation, a spontaneous reaction to the utter and indescribable holiness of Almighty God. It is their unvarnished response to what they behold, a God who is so flawlessly holy! When Isaiah saw this, his reaction was equally telling. He said, "It's all over! I am doomed, for I am a sinful man. I have filthy lips, and I live among a people with filthy lips." God's holiness evoked a similar response in both Isaiah and the Seraphim. The only difference is that the Seraphim did not have a conviction of sin, like Isaiah did. Isaiah was immediately convicted and instinctively knew that he could not approach or stand before this thrice holy God.

In Revelation 4:6-8, we get another glimpse into the throne room of God. We see the four living beings. The first was like a lion; the second like an ox; the third had a human face; and the fourth was like an eagle in flight. Each of these living beings had six wings, and their wings were covered all over with eyes, inside and out. Day after day, and night after night they keep on saying,

> "Holy, holy, holy is the Lord God, the Almighty—the one who always was, who is, and who is still to come."

Here again, we see another part of the heavenly court, the four living beings. They too, like the Seraphim cry continually day and night, holy, holy, holy is the Lord God. The Seraphim and the four living beings could have cried, love, love, love. Or they could have cried powerful, powerful, powerful. They could have cried out any one of the awesome and innumerable qualities that personify and set our God apart. Why is it, that of all the many glorious attributes of God, the one that evokes the cry of the heavenly beings is His holiness?

Holiness is God's total glory crowned.

John McArthur explains, "The holiness of God is not to be conceived of as one attribute among others. It is rather a general term representing the conception of God's consummate perfection and total glory. It is His infinite moral perfection crowning His infinite intelligence and power". McArthur then quotes Thomas Watson who said, "Holiness is the most sparkling jewel of God's crown, it is the name by which He is known"; and R.L. Dabney who said, "Holiness is to be regarded not as a district attribute, but as the result of all God's moral perfection together" (The Holiness of God, McArthur). In other words, Holiness is God's total glory crowned.

Speaking of God, Exodus 15:11 asks rhetorically, "Who is like you, glorious in holiness?" And first Samuel 2:2 says, "There is none holy as the Lord". In the old testament, the term holiness is applied to God in two senses. First, God is separate, set above, and apart from all that is created; and second, things are made or become holy because of their connection with God, for example, holy ground, holy place, and so on.

In sum, God's holiness is the all-consuming, purifying perfection that sanctifies and makes holy, anything that comes in contact with Him. This same holiness can consume and strike dead anyone who approaches God without sanctification (Exodus 19:21-22); or proper decorum (Leviticus 10:1-3). So, because God is so desperately holy, and He created us to have fellowship with Him, He knows that unholiness would, not only bar us from His presence, but would destroy us altogether, hence the loving directive in Hebrews 12:14 to live a holy life because those who are not holy will not "see" or fellowship with God.

The Zeal of The Lord

Zeal is an attribute that we ordinarily associate with humans. People who are driven are seen as zealous, and those who have a fervent commitment to a cause are called zealots. However, the Bible states clearly that God is zealous. In other words, God is "on-fire". Again, and again, the scripture affirms, seals, and confirms a prophecy with this declaration, "The zeal of the Lord of Hosts will perform it" meaning that God will passionately, and relentlessly pursue and vigorously execute that prophecy, to bring it to pass. In Isaiah 9, the prophet Isaiah, after proclaiming the birth of Jesus and describing His many roles, rule and authority, states in verse 7, "Of the increases of his government and peace there shall be no end, upon the throne of David, and upon his kingdom, to order it, and to establish it with judgment and with justice from henceforth even forever. *The zeal of the Lord of Hosts will perform this*".

What is the Zeal of the Lord?

The zeal of the Lord is a holy fire that is heaven-birthed; a righteous indignation and holy anger, a burning passion for righteousness, integrity, truth, and right. The zeal of the Lord is His passion. In Acts 1:3, Jesus's suffering and crucifixion is described as His "passion". The Lord's zeal, "Is a spirit-empowered, heaven-enforcing, devil-crushing anointing that will break the yokes...." (Wanda Alger, Intercessors for America). It is God's "Display of all the divine energy and almighty omnipotence, to accomplish His purpose, to carry out His plan" (The Zeal Of The Lord, C. H. Spurgeon). The zeal of the Lord is revealed and put on display through the manifestations of the character of God.

1. **God's Zeal Displayed Through Perseverance:** We see the zeal of a person when a purpose has been in his or her heart and he or she has followed it through over a long period of time. In the same way, the zeal of God is demonstrated through His determined purpose, and the inexhaustible, infinite, commitment in the mind of God to bring it to pass. The plan of redemption through Jesus Christ was in the heart of God from the beginning of time. In Genesis 3:15, He promised that, "The seed of the woman would bruise the serpent's heel", and in Revelation 13:8, Jesus is described as, "The Lamb slain from the foundation of the world". Through the eons of time, never once did the divine will waver, flag or turn away from this set purpose. He displayed indescribable zeal when He pushed through every obstacle, human sin and failure, and through thousands of years, to bring about the birth, life, death, crucifixion, and resurrection of Jesus. As Isaiah 9:6-7 prophesied seven hundred years prior, "The zeal of the Lord of Hosts" performed it! The zeal of the Lord empowers us to persevere.

2. **God's Zeal Displayed Through Holiness and Sanctification:** In John 2:13-17, when Jesus made a whip and drove money changers out of the temple, His zealous cleansing of the temple prompted His disciples to remember and ascribe to Him the prophecy from the scriptures, "zeal for God's house

146

will consume me." That righteous indignation and holy anger that burned in His spirit and moved him to take action to cleanse the temple is the zeal of the Lord. He could not allow the temple of God to be made unclean and to become a den of thieves. The zeal of the Lord produces holiness and sanctification.

3. **God's Zeal Displayed Through Compassion:** The zeal of the Lord is a holy fire laden with compassion and mercy. It is a zeal for the salvation of souls (Isaiah 37:32). It is our basis for hope, confidence, and ultimate victory in the throes of life. In Isaiah 63:15, the prophet declared, "Lord, look down from heaven; look from your holy, glorious home, and see us. Where is the zeal, passion and the strength you used to show on our behalf? Where are your mercy and compassion now?" According to C. H. Spurgeon, this scripture "Is a battering ram with which to shake the very gates of heaven! Men of prayer and faith, learn how to use this! .....Here is the master plea, "Where is your zeal, and the sounding of your heart?" (*Spurgeon*). The zeal of the Lord moves us with compassion.

4. **God's Zeal Displayed Through Warfare:** The zeal of the Lord's stirs Him up to war against and vanquish His enemies. Whatever challenge threatens the work of the kingdom, whatever temporary defeat appears to stop its advance, we have a sure word of

prophesy, when it's all over, we win! Why? Because the zeal of the Lord of Hosts will perform it. The gates of hell shall not prevail. Isaiah 42:13 states: "The Lord shall go forth like a mighty man; He shall stir up His zeal like a man of war. He shall cry out, yes shout aloud; He shall prevail against His enemies. The zeal of the Lord gives us victory!

C. H. Spurgeon sums it up nicely, "God is not as we are—cold, insensible. He is full of zeal! And in the great good old cause, which shall, at last, win the day, there may be zealous partisans, but none is so zealous as the Lord of Hosts! A Master in the midst of Israel!" "As in the days of battle, when the front ranks are beaten, and one rank after another is driven back, up comes the old guards—and they never quail and know not how to say retreat—and so they win the day! Now behold a greater than all the hosts of men, the eternal ages, the Ancient of days, the infinite, Himself, shall bring up His servants in the day of battle! And He shall thunder gloriously! The gospel shall be proclaimed! The kingdom shall be won! Christ shall reign and the "Hallelujah" shall come up unto the Lord omnipotent, who not only gets the kingdom, but gets it by His own power, wins by His ow zeal! The LORD of hosts, the LORD of hosts shall perform this" (Spurgeon).

The zeal of God is holy fire, blazing in our hearts with passion and commitment. Having this zeal equips us to win in all of life's battles.

Singles and The Zeal of The Lord

God is zealous, and He created, and requires his sons and daughters to be zealous too! Zealous about the plan and purposes of God; completely sold out to and totally in love with Jesus Christ; irrevocably dedicated to the truth and kingdom of God; passionately committed to purity and righteousness; and eternally resolved to hold to no other creed but the Bible, the whole Bible, and nothing but the Bible. This is how God wants us to live. He wants us to be all in, sold out, burn our ships, and leave no room for retreat.

The Bible tells the life story of many singles who lived like this. They were on fire for God and modeled the zeal of the Lord in their daily lives. They were holy, compassionate, long suffering, and victorious. They jealously guarded the fire of God in their hearts and souls. They were WHOLE singles.

Jesus modeled the righteous indignation and zeal of God when He cleansed the temple. He also modeled the limitless compassion and mercy of God. Matthew 9:35-36 tells of how He was moved with compassion for the multitudes, and went about teaching, preaching, and healing all who were sick. And as Acts 1:3 shows, His passionate love for us was put on display on the cross when He died for us. There on that cross, He vanquished the enemy, disarmed principalities and powers, made a public spectacle of them, and triumphed over them (Colossians 2:15). The zeal of the Lord consumed Him.

Apostle Paul was on fire and modeled the exuberant zeal of the Lord. He chose a life of singleness, and set himself apart to live in holiness and consecration to God. In 1 Corinthians 6, he displayed righteous indignation at the sin and immorality in the church and taught Christians that our bodies are the temples of the Holy Spirit. He demonstrated courageous compassion when he put his personal credit on the line to vouch for Onesimus, a runaway slave, and worked to restore the relationship between him and his former master, Philemon (Philemon 1). Paul was constantly at war with the devil and winning! In 2 Corinthians 11:23-29, he described the mind boggling ordeals he encountered and overcame in his commitment to Christ and the work of the kingdom. His passionate zeal burned brightly as he declared, "My old self has been crucified with Christ. It is no longer I who live, but Christ lives in me. So I live in this earthly body by trusting in the son of God, who loved me and gave himself for me" (Galatians 2:20). The zeal of the Lord consumed him!

Daniel was a single man who lived a life that was ablaze for God, and tremendously impacted several heathen kings and their kingdoms. He was a high official in the government of the Medo-Persian empire. He had an excellent spirit and excelled marvelously in everything he did. He rose rapidly in rank among his peers. In Daniel 6:3, the Bible states that, "Daniel soon proved himself more capable than all the other administrators and high officers. Because of Daniel's great ability, the king made plans to place him over the entire empire". When the other administrators, out of jealousy, wanted to find fault with him, the Bible gives this astonishing report, "But they couldn't find anything to criticize or condemn. He was faithful, always responsible, and completely trustworthy. So they concluded, "Our only chance of finding grounds of accusing Daniel will be in connection with the rules of his religion." That was the testimony of his enemies. Wow! What a man!

Daniel was and continues to be an inspiration! His close walk with, and personal commitment to God not only took him to, and victoriously from the lion's den, but it also gave birth to monumental prophetic insights and declarations that provide the blueprint for future world events that would mark the end times, and usher in the return of Jesus Christ. Daniel left an unsullied legacy of righteousness and holy fire that continues to rekindle hearts even today. The Billy Graham Evangelistic Association challenges today's generation to acquire the holy fire of Daniel with their, "Dare to be a Daniel" program. Daniel was an on-fire single, and so also were his friends, Shadrach, Meshack, and Abednego (Daniel 3). The zeal of the Lord consumed them.

Anna was a devout single woman on fire for God. She was married for seven years and became a widow. When we meet her in Luke 2, she was 84 years old, so she had been single most of her life. The Bible states that, "She never left the temple, but stayed there day and night, worshipping God with fasting and prayer" (Luke 2:37). She was a prophetess and recognized baby Jesus as the messiah when His parents brought Him to the temple to dedicate him to the Lord. The Bible declared that she, "Began praising God. She talked about the child to everyone who had been waiting expectantly for God to rescue Jerusalem" (Luke 2:38). The zeal of the Lord consumed her.

Lydia was a business woman from Thyatira, but when we meet her in Acts 16, she was living in Philippi. She was a seller of expensive purple cloth. In Acts 16:13, we learn that Lydia had met with other women, on the sabbath day, at a riverbank for prayer. This is where she ran into apostle Paul and his team. Luke reports, "As she listened to us, the Lord opened her heart, and she accepted what Paul was saying" (Acts 16:14). After she believed, she and her household were baptized and she became a supporter of the ministry. She insisted that Paul, Silas, Timothy, and Luke stay at her home. Her insistence indicates the fervency of her desire to serve them and support their ministry. She said to them, "If you agree that I am a true believer in the Lord, come and stay at my home" (Acts 16:15), and they did. Lydia is the first person recorded to have been saved in Europe. The zeal of the Lord consumed her!

Martha was a well to do, hardworking and accomplished woman. We are first introduced to her in Luke

10:38. The scripture tells us that Martha had her own home, where she lived with her sister Mary. In the Bible, a woman having her own home in a society where women had no property or inheritance rights speaks volumes about her dexterity, ability, and work ethic. Martha invited Jesus to her home where she hosted Him and His disciples. In John 11, we see Martha's reaction when her brother died and Jesus did not show up when she expected him to. Naturally, she expressed disappointment that Jesus had not come earlier to heal Lazarus, but she did not stop there. She said "Lord, if you had been here, my brother would not have died. But even now, I know that God will give you whatever you ask". She had faith in the power of Jesus to heal and when Jesus transitioned to talking about resurrection power, she affirmed her faith in Him. She said, "Yes, Lord, I have always believed you are the Messiah, the Son of God, the one who has come into the world from God." Again, in John 12, six days before the Passover, when a dinner party was held in Jesus's honor at the home of Lazarus, Martha served. Every time we see Martha, she is serving. The zeal of the Lord consumed her.

All these single men and women were not slinking, diffident, abashed, timid, or apologetic individuals. Rather, they were fiery, purposeful, and impassioned people who served the Lord with single minded devotion and zeal. They were not self-absorbed people, putting their lives on hold, focused only on getting married, and resentful against the Lord because they are single. They were men and women on a mission to impact their world for the kingdom of God. Their singleness was an opportunity, a tool of service, to honor God, and build His kingdom. God wants us to live like that.

Restoration of Holy Fire

Every Christian single can and should be on fire for God. The single men and women in the Bible amply illustrate this point. This chapter has outlined the many challenges that can beset, ambush, and quench the fire of God in our hearts. But we must not let it! The fire of God is precious. It is to be jealously guarded and faithfully tended in our lives. We must not let the fire go out. In 2 Timothy 1:6, apostle Paul challenged Timothy to, "Fan into flames the spiritual gift God gave you when I laid my hands on you". This exhortation acknowledges the reality that we need to tend the fire of God in our lives and when it begins to burn low, fan it into roaring flames.

God has invested so much in His single sons and daughters. We must contend earnestly for the treasure that He has put in us. "We are like fragile clay jars containing this great treasure. This makes clear that our great power is from God, not from ourselves" (2 Corinthians 4:7). So, to maintain and manifest this treasure within us, we must cultivate the presence of

God. We must restore holy fire in our lives. How do we do that?

1. **Lay it Down:** Present before God, as a sacrificial offering, your deepest desire as a single Christian. Whether it is the desire to be married, to have children, to serve with your future spouse in Christian ministry, and so on, offer it to God, the same way Abraham offered Isaac. When we lay our deepest desires before God as a sacrifice, it is:

   a. A declaration of His Lordship over us.

   b. Confirmation that He is the primary focus of our lives.

   c. Evidence of our surrender to His will and plan for us.

   d. An affirmation of our trust in Him and His love and care for us.

   e. Declaration of our submission to His timing.

   f. An act of worship. When we lay our deepest desires on the altar, it is consecrated to the Lord, and the fire of God will fall and consume that sacrifice.

g. Disarms the devil, who always tries to drive a wedge between us and God, using unfulfilled desires. When we offer our unfulfilled desires to God, the devil loses the battle. When we say like Job, "Though He slay me, yet will I trust Him" (Job 13:15), the devil loses his ability to use our unfulfilled desires to slander God to us.

2. **Get Up and Out:** Stop rehearsing your disappointments and failures, that will only lead to resentment. Recognize that what happened to you explains why you are where you are, but is no reason for you to stay there. Determine in your heart to get up and out! This does not mean that you can snap your fingers and "be happy". What it does mean is that you can partner with the Holy Spirit to execute the divine exchange described in Isaiah 61:1-3. He can take your ashes and give you His beauty; exchange your spirit of grief and mourning, with His joy; and help you to put on the garment of praise when the spirit of heaviness tries to overtake you. Note that praise is a garment, and so, you have to put it on. Just like your clothes don't just "jump" on you, but you have to put them on, in the same way, when the spirit of grief and heaviness tries to come upon you, you have to make a conscious choice to put on the garment of praise, by turning on praise music, singing, and thanking God. Though at the outset, you may still feel downcast, as you continue to

praise God, you will pierce the darkness of depression, and mount up on the wings of praise above the bitterness and heaviness of your disappointments.

*Hope is a confident expectation that God will
do what He said He will do.*

3. **Rekindle Hope:** Hope is a confident expectation that God will do what He said He will do. Has God made you a promise? Have you been standing on the word of God for a long time? Do you feel disappointed and disillusioned? I challenge you to rekindle your hope. Do not cast away your confidence. God will keep His word to you. He made an appointment with you when He gave you His word, and He will keep that appointment, no matter what.

Most people skip the genealogies in the Bible. This is the long list of names that trace the ancestral lineage of a person. However, one of the most hope-building scriptures in the entire Bible is the genealogy recorded in Matthew 1:1. After a long list of names, verse 17 summarizes, "So all the generations from Abraham to David are fourteen generations; and from David until the carrying away into Babylon are fourteen generations; and from the carrying away into Babylon unto Christ are fourteen generations."

There were altogether forty two generations spanning more than a thousand years from Abraham to Jesus Christ. In this intervening period, was a multitude of human sin and failure; including incest, murder, adultery, prostitution, and so on. But neither the passage of time, human failure, or the devil himself could stop the promise of God to send a savior. Galatians 4:4 states, "But when the right time came, God sent his Son, born of a woman." Who knew the right time? God did, and He kept a tab on the time. Each segment of time was fourteen generations exactly. God did not miss a beat, but you couldn't see it in the moment; only in hindsight. Same thing with you. God is watching over His word in your life to perform it. He is Jehovah nick-of-time. He knows the right time to bring His promises to pass. Trust Him.

4. **Take Responsibility:** Own your part in creating the disappointments you have experienced. Let me explain. It is the weight that we attach to anything that gives it the power to disappoint and crush us. In other words, it is the large premium that you place on getting married, having children, and so on, that makes your current single status such a devastating blow. Reassess your own value system and challenge how much value you attach to the things that have disappointed and disillusioned you. This does not mean that you stop wanting to be married, but it does mean that you surrender

the timing, anxiety and worry about it to the Lord, and leave it there. It's like the apostle Paul. When he became immersed in Christ, the result was a striking reassessment and shift in his value system. In Philippians 3:7-8, after recounting his pedigree, achievements and accolades in the natural, he said "I once thought these things were valuable, but now I consider them worthless because of what Christ has done. Yes everything else is worthless when compared with the infinite value of knowing Christ Jesus my Lord. For his sake I have discarded everything else, counting it all as garbage, so that I could gain Christ and become one with him."

5. **Fasting and Prayer**: Seeking God in fasting and prayer will rekindle your fire, and drench your soul with His refreshing. There is nothing quite like spending time alone with God to renew your strength, ignite your fire, and clarify your focus (Isaiah 40:31). When my soul is frazzled, distracted, discontented, and disquieted within me, I step away and spend time seeking the face of the Lord. Every single time, the Lord Himself is my reward. When I bask in His presence, He floods and saturates my being with Himself, stills my soul, quietens my heart, and confirms my faith and trust in His working, and timing in my life.

> *Victory comes when you say the same thing about yourself, that God says about you!*

6. **Proclaim the Word:** The spoken word of God is our offensive weapon. It is the sword of the Spirit. Revelation 12:11 states, "And they overcame him (the devil) by the blood of the Lamb and by the word of their testimony". In Mark 11:23, Jesus said, "I say to you, whoever says to this mountain, 'Be removed and be cast into the sea,' and does not doubt in his heart, but believes that those things he says will be done, he will have whatever he says." You cannot overestimate the power of the spoken word. The word of God is filled with the creative power of God, and the Zoë life of God. It will rekindle holy fire in your soul, and fill you with abundant life. This is how we fight our battles. This is how we win! So, to restore holy fire, take the word of God in your mouth and speak it forth. Victory comes when you say the same thing about yourself, that God says about you!

7. **Trust in God's Plan and Timing**: When your heart gets weary from waiting, remind yourself that God knows you by name, sees you, knows exactly where you are, and hears the cry of your heart. Affirming your trust in God will rekindle holy fire in your soul. God cares personally, intimately, and passionately

for you. He has you on His mind twenty four hours a day. Psalm 139:17-18 states, "How precious are your thoughts about me, O God. They cannot be numbered! I can't even count them; they outnumber the grains of sand! And when I wake up, you are still with me!" You are always on the mind of your heavenly Father. Have you been waiting long for God? Don't grow weary. He is mightily at work on your behalf. Isaiah 64:4 states, "For since the world began no ear has heard and no eye has seen a God like you, who works for those who wait for him!" One of the names of God that is not in the Bible is Jehovah nick-of-time. God often comes, just in the nick of time. He is never in a hurry, but He is never late. He will perfect all that concerns you – Amen.

8. **Find Purpose Beyond Yourself, Invest Yourself in Others**: One sure fire way to rekindle the fire of God in your heart, is to take your eyes off of yourself and become "others focused". Helping other people will never fail to heal, restore, and give you a fresh sense of purpose. Focusing on yourself and what you don't have, is not only depressing, but it can lead to ingratitude and an obsession. That territory is the devil's stomping ground. Regardless of what is presently lacking in your life, you have so much to be thankful for. Helping others reminds you of how blessed you are, and prompts you to give thanks for what you do have. When you help others, you

multiply joy by giving joy; plus, you gain a sense of purpose and blessing that reinvigorates you. This is because God created you to be a blessing, so blessing others gives you a sense of wellbeing, and fulfills one of your primary assignments on the earth.

The Power of a Personal Altar

It is impossible to be on-fire for God without a personal altar. In fact, an altar-less Christian is a powerless Christian. To restore holy fire in your life, you must prepare an altar where the fire of God can fall. An altar is a time and/or place that is sanctified or set apart for God. It is a time and/or place where you meet with God. In Exodus 20:23-24, God said to the Children of Israel, "Remember, you must not make any idols of silver or gold to rival me. Build for me an altar made of earth.....Build my altar wherever I cause my name to be remembered, and I will come to you and bless you."

Here God is saying, if you want to meet with me, don't make an image, raise an altar. Altars are very significant in spiritual warfare. It is a gateway into the supernatural. If you prepare and set apart a time and place to meet with God, you are most likely to have divine encounters at that time and place. An altar is a place of invocation. It is a place of activation or servicing of covenants. It is a place of worship, sacrifice, blessing, refuge, and protection (Exodus 20:24; 1 Kings 1:50-53; 2:28-29).

> *An altar-less Christian*
> *is a powerless Christian.*

In the Old Testament, men raised physical stone altars. Abraham raised several altars to the Lord. So did Isaac and Jacob (Genesis 28:1-22). In the New Testament, believers in Jesus are themselves the temples of God and our heart is his altar (Corinthians 6:19-2). So, to set up a personal altar, all you need to do is to establish a time and/or place, consecrate it to the Lord, make a commitment to the Lord to meet with Him there, and then, follow through.

Blessings of the Altar

There are many blessings of a personal altar. In Exodus 20:24, God promised that if you set up an altar, He will come to you and bless you. So, the first blessing of a personal altar is the presence of God. In addition, a Christian with a personal altar will experience progressive brokenness, holiness, and consecration. By setting up an altar, you are saying, "Lord, I give you my full attention." God in turn responds in the words of Jeremiah 29:13, "If you seek me, you will find me when you search for me with all your heart". When you raise an altar, it is a personal invitation to Almighty God, and He will show up every single time.

A personal altar is a declaration of dependence on God, and an acknowledgment of His ownership and Lordship over your life. It cultivates the presence of God, and an ability to hear, and recognize His voice. Also, altars sharpen spiritual perception and discernment (Romans 12:2; Acts 16:16-19). It is a place to receive divine guidance, and for the display or manifestation of the power of God (1 Kings 18:30-39). For the New Testament Christian, an altar is a place to activate, appropriate, and deploy the finished works of Christ!

Several years ago, I heard a story that illustrated, so pointedly, the power of a personal altar. It is the story of a young ruffian who gave his life to Christ. This guy was a member of a motorcycle gang, and was into all manner of drugs, sin, and debauchery. His body was a walking billboard of tattoos. He was a rude, crude, leud, dude. Then he met Jesus. He did not have a Christian background and had never been to church. He worked a construction job, and there was a little old church near the construction site. So, every afternoon at lunch time, he would go to the church. The first time he went there, nobody was there. He sat in the back, fidgeted a little, cleared his throat a couple times and awkwardly said, "Jesus, man, I think you are cool. I just want to say, it's really been great knowing you". He didn't know what else to say, so, he sat for a little while longer, and left. Every day at lunch time, he would make his daily trip to the church to talk to Jesus. Unbeknownst to him, the pastor of the church had been observing him from the vestry. The first time he came, the pastor was apprehensive, and wondered whether he had come to perpetrate some felony at the church. But after he came a couple times, the pastor introduced himself, chatted with him for a while, and heard the young man's story about how he had lived the life of a prodigal and how Jesus saved him. He told him he was welcome to the church anytime.

After a while, the young man stopped coming. A week passed, and the pastor got concerned. So, he went to the construction site to inquire, and found out that the young man had fallen from a scaffolding and was in the hospital. The pastor went to visit him. When he came into his hospital room, he saw a chair pulled up against the bed, like someone had been visiting. He knew from his discussion with the young man that his lifestyle had alienated his family, and he was estranged from his parents. It was unlikely that anybody would visit him in the hospital. So, he asked him, "looks like you've had visitors?" The young man with tears in his eyes told the pastor that every day, at lunch time, Jesus came to visit and sat in that Chair. He would call him by name and say to him, "man, I think you are cool. I just want to say, it's really been great knowing you".

This is the power of a personal altar. It brings the presence of God. The young man did not know it, but he had set up a personal altar with the Lord, and when he couldn't come to the church, Jesus kept that appointment and came to him in the hospital. The rest of the story is that while his accident was very serious, and he had been expected to die or have permanent disability from his fall, he was miraculously healed by the love and grace of God.

The Fellowship of the Unashamed

Are you on-fire for God? If not, are you ready for the restoration of holy fire in your life? Are you all-in and sold out, or do you have a plan B? Are you a follower or a fan? Are you a disciple of Jesus Christ? Are you part of the fellowship of the unashamed?

In 1980, a Rwandan man was being forced by his tribe to either renounce Christ or face certain death. He refused to renounce Christ, and was killed. The night before, he had written a personal commitment which he titled, "The Fellowship of the Unashamed", which was later found in his room. Since then, this fierce declaration has been adopted by, and has become the creed of Christians worldwide who are all-in and on-fire for Christ. If that describes you, then read this, let it sink into your soul and become your personal declaration of commitment.

I am part of the "Fellowship of the Unashamed."
The die has been cast. I have stepped over the line.
The decision has been made. I am a disciple of
Jesus Christ. I won't look back, let up, slow down,

back away, or be still. My past is redeemed,
my present
makes sense, and my future is secure.
I am finished and done with low living, sight walking,
small planning, smooth knees, colorless dreams,
chintzy giving, and dwarfed goals.

I no longer need pre-eminence, prosperity, position,
promotions, plaudits, or popularity. I now live by
presence, lean by faith, love by patience,
lift by prayer, and labor by power. My pace
is set, my gait is fast, my goal is Heaven, my
road is narrow, my way is rough, my companions few,
my Guide reliable, my mission clear. I cannot
be bought,
compromised, deterred, lured away, turned back,
diluted, or delayed.

I will not flinch in the face of sacrifice, hesitate in the
presence of adversity, negotiate at the table of
the enemy,
ponder at the pool of popularity, or meander
in the maze of mediocrity.

I am a disciple of Jesus Christ. I must go until
Heaven returns, give until I drop, preach
until all know,
and work until He comes. And when He comes to get
His own, He will have no problem recognizing me.
My colors will be clear.

As I wrote this chapter, the Holy Spirit brought to my memory a short chorus written long ago by Rosemary Hilvers. When I was a teenager, I sang this song with deep conviction, as a declaration of my passionate commitment to Christ. I challenge you to speak the words of this song as a prayer over yourself, make it your personal declaration and regularly proclaim it over yourself.

> The zeal of God has consumed me
> It burns within my soul
> A driving force that cannot be stopped
> A fire that cannot be quenched

Present yourself to the Lord and consecrate your life, including this season of singleness, to Him. His holy fire will fall and set your heart ablaze.

Singleness is Good

Many Christian singles are discontented with their single status because deep within their hearts, they believe that singleness is not good. They pine for marriage and lose their zeal for life and God, because they feel left out, lonely, and dissatisfied. However, the Bible states expressly that singleness is not only good, but in many instances, it is better than marriage, and is specially blessed by God. To maintain holy fire, it is important that Christian singles see their singleness through the eyes of God.

1. **Singleness is a Good and Recommended Choice:** Several times in the Bible, apostle Paul, who was single all his life, recommended a single lifestyle over marriage. In 1 Corinthians 7:7-8, he states, "I wish everyone were single, just as I am. So I say to those who aren't married and to widows—it's better to stay unmarried, just as I am." Here, Paul, the foremost apostle, who wrote most of the New Testament, clearly states that a single lifestyle is better than marriage.

2. **Do Not Seek to Get Married:** First Corinthians 7:25-28 states, "Now regarding your question about the young women who are not yet married. I do not have a command from the Lord for them. But the Lord in his mercy has given me wisdom that can be trusted, and I will share it with you. ... I think it is best to remain as you are. If you have a wife, do not seek to end the marriage. If you do not have a wife, do not seek to get married. But if you do get married, it is not a sin. And if a young woman gets married, it is not a sin." Did you see that? Apostle Paul said, "Do not seek to get married." Quite a different message from what singles routinely hear from the culture and the church, that if you are not married, something is wrong with you. So, singles

feel compelled to seek, pursue, and go after marriage by hook or by crook.

3. **Marriage Brings with It Troubles and Challenges:** Marriage has its own troubles and challenges that the unmarried and single can do without. First Corinthians 7:28b states, "Those who get married at this time will have troubles, and I am trying to spare you those problems." Unlike the starry eyed day-dream that many singles have and nurture in their hearts, of marriage fixing all their problems, the reality is that marriage is fraught with its own unique difficulties. So, marriage is not a panacea, it is trading one set of challenges for another. Often, the grass looks greener on the other side of the fence, but it rarely is.

4. **Singleness Provides Many Advantages:** First Corinthians 7:32-40 outlines the many advantages of a single lifestyle:

   a. Freedom from the concerns of this life.

   b. An unmarried man can spend his time doing the Lord's work and thinking about how to please God. But a married man has to think about his earthly responsibilities and how to please his wife. His interests are divided.

c.   In the same way, an unmarried woman can be fully devoted to the Lord and holy in body and spirit. But a married woman has to think about her earthly responsibilities and how to please her husband.

d.   Singleness confers a benefit. Apostle Paul says, I am saying "don't marry" for your benefit, not to place restrictions on you.

e.   Singleness will help you serve the Lord best, with as few distractions as possible.

5. **Singleness is Even Better Than Marriage:** First Corinthians 7:38 states, "So, the person who marries his fiancée does well, and the person who doesn't marry does *even better.*" This scripture is saying that in this situation, singleness is *even better* than marriage!

6. **Counsel of God's Spirit, Better to Stay Single:** First Corinthians 7:40 states, "In my opinion it would be better for her to stay single, and I think I am giving you counsel from God's Spirit when I say this." Note that the counsel from God's Spirit in this instance is that it is better to stay single. This passage illustrates that the undue pressure placed on all singles to get married is wrong. The legitimate counsel of the Holy Spirit for some may be to

stay single. An example is the prophet Jeremiah who was expressly directed by God not to marry (Jeremiah 16:1-2).

7. **God Has a Special Blessing for Singles:** Isaiah 46:4-5 states, "For this is what the Lord says: I will bless those eunuchs who keep my Sabbath days holy and who choose to do what pleases me and commit their lives to me. I will give them—within the walls of my house— a memorial and a name far greater than sons and daughters could give. For the name I give them is an everlasting one. It will never disappear!" This scripture stipulates a special blessing for singles who honor God, and commit themselves to live lives that please Him. God promises to give them a memorial and an everlasting name, which shall never disappear. So many singles execute different types of maneuvers to gain the name, husband or wife. But here, God promises to give every God-honoring single an everlasting name, far better than and superior to the title, Mr. & Mrs.

Singleness is a Valid Option

We live in a sex-crazed world. So even though the godly option of singleness is clearly in the bible, you would never hear this type of teaching from most pulpits. The emphasis is always on marriage as though that is the only option. However, the bible presents singleness as a credible, legitimate, and blessed option. In Matthew 19:11-12, Jesus taught that there are three types of adult singleness:

1. Some are born as eunuchs (Natural Eunuchs)

2. Some have been made eunuchs by others (Forced Eunuchs), and

3. Some choose not to marry for the sake of the Kingdom of Heaven. (Voluntary Eunuchs)

While the word eunuch was used specifically for males, this teaching of Jesus about singleness applies equally to women. Natural eunuchs include those who are born with no real desire for marriage or sex; as well as those who were born with a physical sexual defect or malfunction that obviates the need for sex. In today's world, it could also include people whose sexual desire have been permanently impacted by testicular cancer.

Forced eunuchs are those who have been castrated for whatever reason. The castration procedure was intended to make the subject asexual, disinterested in sex, lacking a sexual urge and unable to produce children. It was a common practice in ancient times for rulers to castrate men who tended to the royal harem. This was to ensure that they did not engage in sexual activity with the royal wives, or develop romantic interests that might tempt them towards betrayal. Esther

4:4 mentions Esther's eunuchs. And Acts 8:26-40 tells the story of the Ethiopian eunuch, who was a high court official of Candace the queen of Ethiopia. Of note, some eunuchs were castrated as punishment for sexual crimes.

Voluntary eunuchs are those who, in order to better serve the Lord in some capacity, choose to forgo marriage and remain celibate. (*What is a Eunuch, gotquestions.org*).

Apostle Paul was a voluntary eunuch. He chose a single and celibate lifestyle so he can devote himself to serve the Lord without distractions. In 1 Corinthians 7, he repeatedly urged believers to follow his example and choose singleness.

While it is clear from the scriptures that Daniel was never married, it is not clear whether he was castrated or was a voluntary eunuch. He served in Babylon at a time when many servants in the royal court were castrated, and the Bible states that he served under the chief of the eunuchs, a man named Aspenaz. However, there is no direct statement as to whether or not he was castrated. What is clear is that he lived a life that was wholly devoted to the Lord, as a single man, and made an eternal impact in the lives of future generations.

Jeremiah was a man called by God from birth to serve as a prophet. His forty year ministry spanned some of the most difficult times in the history of the nation of Israel. He prophesied from the thirteenth year of king Josiah's reign till the fall of Jerusalem.

He faced formidable opponents who tried to silence him by threats, intimidation, arrests, beatings, imprisonments, and even assassination plots (Jeremiah 26:10-19, 36:26; 37:11-38:6). Jeremiah did not marry because God told him not to marry. In Jeremiah 16:1-2, the prophet states, "The Lord gave me another message. He said, "Do not get married or have children in this place." Jeremiah's entire life was focused on fulfilling God's prophetic agenda for the nation of Israel. He left a rich legacy of faithful, sacrificial and courageous service to God.

Singleness Provides a Unique Opportunity

Singleness provides a unique opportunity to serve the Lord passionately and whole heartedly, without let, hindrance, or distraction. A single man or woman can make Christ their primary focus and single-mindedly devote themselves to establishing the kingdom of God. They can commit to projects, assignments, and kingdom initiatives that they may not be able to do, if they were married or have children. Simply stated, a single person can dedicate more time to building the kingdom of God.

In John 9:4, Jesus said, "I must work the works of Him who sent Me while it is day; the night is coming when no one can work." Jesus made this statement in the context of His limited time on earth to accomplish His redemptive assignment. But this scripture so aptly describes the opportunities we have to accomplish the purposes of God during distinct seasons of our lives. Jesus's season to walk the earth in a human body was limited and He maintained a strict focus on accomplishing and finishing His mission.

Our season of singleness is equally limited, and a focused single man or woman who is on-fire for God can achieve so much more for the kingdom of God than a married person can. Apostle Paul illustrated this with his own life, and challenged us to emulate him. He noted that a married man or woman has troubles and distractions associated with meeting the needs of their spouse and family; whereas a single person is unburdened by these encumbrances. Note that for single parents, this is often not the case, because they have the responsibility of raising their kids, sometimes, all alone.

For some kingdom assignments, "night" may come when you get married and have children. For example, before I was married, I could readily go on mission trips, but when I got married and became a mom, and later, a single mom, night came for me in that area. I still support mission trips financially, and serve as an online missionary with a global missions organization. But with a kid in grade school, my opportunities to physically travel for mission trips are few and far between.

A single person can choose to devote more of their time to prayer and the study of the word. Without a mate to cater for and children to raise, a single person can make a strong commitment to word study, prayer, and ministry. A single person can go back to school to earn a degree, go to bible school, begin a new hobby, travel the world, learn a musical instrument, serve their community and so on. A married person can too, but the challenges, burden, and distractions are multiplied.

In my book, *Choosing a Life of Victory*, I tell the story of Erin Kline, a beautiful young woman who is currently single. Speaking of the opportunity afforded by her single status, Erin said, "This is only a season; therefore, my aim is to be content with the season I am in because I know it's only temporary. There is a reason that I'm still single, so rather than dwelling on what I don't have right now or what may be missing from my life, I'm taking advantage of the opportunity afforded by my singleness and embracing what I do have and where I am now. I can do certain things to prepare for marriage, but in the meantime, there is plenty else to be done. Sometimes I think I can do so much now because I *am* single. I'm at a time in my life where I can pour myself into my job, my friends, and family, as well as the outreach ministry that I lead at my church (REACH) because I have the time. I know when I'm married and have kids, I won't be able to do all of this, or at least to the extent that I do now because my focus and priorities will shift. My time of being single has allowed me to grow and do things that I might not have otherwise been able to do had I been married" (Godson).

How to Successfully Engage
Your Season of Singleness

Whether you are single for a period of years or single your entire life, in the context of eternity, your singleness is a season, and how you engage your season of singleness will determine the outcome and impact of your life! You can spend your time sulking and feeling sorry for yourself, or you can actively engage and change your world! One thing is clear, we will give account to God for the single seasons of our lives.

In Matthew 25:14-30, Jesus told the parable of the talents. The master gave one servant, five talents; the other, two talents; and the last servant, one talent. While the servants with five and two talents worked hard and invested their talents, the servant with one talent went and hid his talent. He had an excuse, he was resentful toward the master, but that did not exonerate him. When the master came back, his judgment was harsh and His sentence swift. "He ordered, 'take the talent from this servant, and give it to the one with the ten talents. To those who use well what they are given, even more will be given, and they will have an abundance. But from those who did nothing, even what little they have will be taken away. Now throw this useless servant into outer darkness where there will be weeping and gnashing of teeth"

Sadly, this is the tale of so many Christian singles. They believe that they have been given one talent. They are not married like so and so. Others appear to have the perfect life, the married life they so desperately want and pray for. Like the one talent guy, they feel resentful. They feel that life has given them a raw deal. Some feel that God has disappointed them. They have lived a good life and served God faithfully, but things didn't turn out as they hoped. They did not expect to be single at this time in their lives, or for this long. Others have become single again through traumatic events, and they feel that those events were unfair. Maybe they prayed and believed for their spouse to be healed, and they died anyway; or they had been a faithful spouse, who believed that their marriage commitment was for life, but instead, they were blindsided by infidelity, separation or divorce.

> *It doesn't matter what you have, it matters only what you do with what you have.*

Well, being resentful towards the master was not a good excuse for the one talent guy, nor is it for us, as singles. You see, like that guy, God has invested so much in us. Jesus died to save us and gave us His Spirit to impact our world. Every Christian single has the best "one talent" in the world; the precious Holy Spirit living inside us; the same Spirit that raised Jesus Christ from the dead! We can choose to make excuses or we can get to work. But one thing is sure, one day, we will be required to give an account of what we did with our season of singleness. Like the one talent guy, it will never work for us to say to the master, "I put my life on hold, because I was waiting to get married." That is the same thing the one talent guy did. The excuse may be different, but the outcome is the same. Both talents are buried and not invested in the kingdom. It is hard to imagine the master's judgement being any different for us than it was for him.

Every Christian single has the best "one talent" in the world; The precious Holy Spirit!

---

1. He took the talent from him and gave it to the guy who was busy. Has it ever occurred to you that God never gives anything worthwhile to anybody who is idle? In fact, every person Jesus called, was busy working. Peter, James, and John, were fishing; Matthew was collecting taxes; Simon was a zealot, and so on. It seemed that Jesus could stand just about anybody, sinners, prostitutes, tax collectors, and so on, except indolent people. He called busy people and then He gave them more work to do. We think differently. We think, "Give the work to the man who has nothing to do". But Jesus doesn't do that. He is interested in productive people. It doesn't matter to Him what you have, it matters

only what you do with what you have. He will never ask of us what He did not give us. He said expressly to us, "Occupy till I come" (Luke 19:13). We must be about the master's business. Singles don't get a free pass because we are single. If anything, we have more time and opportunity. We can choose to invest or squander it. Note that the Bible says in Matthew 12:36, that we will give account for every idle word that we speak. That is how much God dislikes idleness. We will account for every idle or non-working word we speak. If we will give account for idle words, He will certainly require us to give account for unproductive seasons of our lives.

God is at work in your life and all around you, join Him!

2. The one talent guy did not take responsibility for his life. He did what many singles do today. They blame the outcomes of their lives on someone else. Their ex-spouse, ex-boy or girlfriend, ex-boss, or on the Lord, who didn't answer their prayer for a spouse. That ruse did not work for the one talent guy, and it will not work for any Christian single. As an adult, it is your responsibility to tend to your own life. It's a waste of precious time and energy to obsess over being single. Determine to take your eyes off

yourself, and to act on purpose, and with intentionality to impact your world, and transform the lives of people in your sphere of influence. God wants you to live a life of purpose, passion, and power. He is at work in your life and all around you. Join Him! He knows exactly where you are and will bring your spouse to you where you are at work. Notice that He brought the additional talents to the five talent guy where he was at work.

3. Doing nothing with your talent produces bitterness and multiplies resentment. The derelict servant did nothing with his talent, so, his one talent remained one talent. At the same time, the five talent guy had grown his five talents to ten, and the two talent guy had multiplied his talents to four. Notice that the gap is widening between the one talent guy and his colleagues who were at work. Notice also that when the master came, the derelict servant did most of the talking. He had nothing to show for his wasted years, so, he complained about the master. If the master had allowed him to continue talking, he would have moved on to the two and five talent guys; and waxed eloquent about how arrogant they were; and how they thought they were better than everybody else; and how things always worked out for them; after all, they started out with so much more than he did. That is the loser's croon. Losers take little, if any, responsibility for their lives. They disclaim responsibility

for their choices and blame others. But like the one talent guy, their whining and envy does not confuse the master. He sees it for what it is. A thin cover for their laziness. Your rotten lot in life or what people did to you may be the reason why you are the way you are, but do not use it as an excuse to stay that way. Your future is your responsibility.

Your future is your responsibility.

---

4. Think about it, if the one talent guy could not produce a profit from only one talent, how could he ever hope to be useful to the master? The scripture says that they were given talents according to their ability. The two talent guy did not bemoan his two talents, accuse the master or envy the guy with five. He simply put his two talents to work. But the one talent guy did not. In Luke 16:10-12, Jesus taught an important principle, "If you are unfaithful in little things, you will be unfaithful in large ones. But if you are dishonest in little things, you won't be honest with greater responsibilities. And if you are untrustworthy about worldly wealth, who will trust you with the true riches of heaven? And if you are unfaithful with other people's things, why should you be trusted with things of your own?"

This principle has direct application here. If you as a single person cannot manage your own life, and invest your time to be productive for the kingdom of God, why would God give you a spouse or family to care for? Why would God give you more responsibility when you have demonstrated that you are not capable of handling your own life? If you bemoan your single status, envy your married friends, and refuse to serve others, why would God give you a family to serve? Marriage and family is all about self-sacrifice and service. If you cannot give of yourself and your time to serve people in your church or community, why would God give you a family to serve? Maybe God has not given you your spouse yet, because you have not completed your single assignment. So, get to work!

5. The one talent guy wanted to control the outcome. He had one talent, he was afraid of the master, so he wanted to ensure that he incurred no loss. He did not want to take any risk of loss, and by ensuring no risk of loss, he also gave up the potential upside. You see, risk is like a pendulum that swings both ways. It has the downside potential for loss and pain, but it also has the upside potential for gain and joy. The problem is, there are no guarantees; investment requires risk. It requires giving up control. It requires effort and faith that the outcome will justify the investment. This was a bridge too

far for the one talent guy. Even though he blamed his master, the fault was much deeper and very personal. He did not have enough faith in himself to invest his talent in his own future. So, he settled for the status quo.

> *Maybe God has not given you*
> *your spouse, because you have not*
> *completed your single assignment.*

This is the story of so many singles who are unwilling to take any risk. We want to control the outcome, to preserve our one talent, to play it safe. We isolate ourselves because we don't want to risk being hurt by others. We say "no" to new relationships out of fear. We do not want to be vulnerable. We think, "What if it doesn't work out?" So, we hide in plain sight. We do not associate or connect with new things or new people. Yet, no good thing comes without a risk. I challenge you to get out there and connect with others, because in connecting with others, you discover yourself. Don't wait, start today.

Other singles put their lives on hold. They want to do many things for the Lord, but only after they find "the one". It is as if; if they take their eyes off of getting married for just one minute, they would miss their soul mate. You see, the job of finding them a soul mate is too big for God, so they have to do it themselves. They have to stay up, watch vigilantly, and keep their eyes peeled. They cannot afford to be distracted by serving God or other people, and risk missing "the one".

These singles are so fixated on getting married, that they are missing both the point and fun of just being alive! They mortgage today and miss out on today's joys, because they are fixated on tomorrow, a specific type of tomorrow; one with a particular type of spouse, and two and a half kids. They miss out on great opportunities to make their lives more rich, interesting, fruitful, and impactful today. Psalm 127:1 warns us against this self-help approach to life. It states, "Unless the Lord builds a house, the work of the builders is wasted."

6. The master consigns the servant to outer darkness, a place of punishment and gnashing of teeth, not because he had one talent, but because he was useless and unproductive. This is instructive. It is the same reason Jesus cursed the fig tree in Mark 11:12-14. From a distance, it was in "full leaf", giving an appearance of fruitfulness, but when Jesus came closer and looked for fruit on it, it was unproductive. It was all leaves and no fruit.

It's almost comical. The one talent guy was complaining that life was hard because he had only one talent, but his situation got worse in a hurry. He ended up, not only having zero talent, but in prison as well. This is where complaining and an unproductive lifestyle always leads, to poverty and captivity. Make no mistake, we will give account for what we do with our season of singleness.

Invest in Eternity

By far, the greatest trust God has placed in us is the stewardship of our time. God lives in eternity, but we live in time, and God has given us stewardship of our time. Time is the most precious commodity we have. Our lives are made up of seconds and minutes. Everyone gets the exact same amount of time. Every day, we each get 24 hours to spend, invest or squander as we choose. And the next day, the same. When we go to work, we are paid for our time. Some people describe it as "putting in our time". Each paycheck is essentially payment for a portion of our lives that we will never be able to live again. We traded those hours in for cash. Same thing with the rest of our lives, some of us trade it in for worthless trifles, while others invest it for eternal impact. Take a Friday night for example, some people will squander it on frivolous fritters, a few hours at a bar, illicit sex, gambling or some other fleeting past time; others will "kill time" with mindless television binge watching; while others will invest it in a wholesome evening with their children and family; or serving the poor and needy at a homeless shelter; or coaching young boys who do not have a dad in their lives. The same time, invested very differently, with very different impacts and outcomes, some trivial, and others eternal.

Our lives are meted out to us in 24 hour increments. We are not told how many 24 hour installments we will have, only to be judicious and wise in how we spend each allotment of time we get. One thing about time, once we spend it, we can never get it back. 8am of today is gone, and until I die, I will never again re-live 8am of April 10th, 2019. It is gone forever, and anything I did not do at 8am today, I will never again, until I die, do it at 8am of April 10th, 2019. Soon, this day will be gone forever, and all that is left are memories. One day, our time on earth will be over and there will be an obituary or cemetery somewhere that tells a short story about our lives. Typically, it will give the deceased's name, the year of their birth, a little dash, and then the year of their death. A little dash, that's all it is. Think of the brevity of it, just a little dash. That little dash is the sum total of our lives, whether we lived a hundred years or 10 years doesn't matter. What matters is what we did with our dash. My challenge to you today is to invest your dash in serving others and building the kingdom of God.

Your single season is a precious gift from God. Invest this time with eternity in view. Below is a poem about time that made a big impact on me. Read it, consider and ponder it, and let it motivate you to live a fruitful and productive single life.

The Value Of Time

Imagine there is a bank account that credits your account each morning with $86,400. It carries over no balance from day to day. Every evening the bank deletes whatever part of the balance you failed to use during the day. What would you do? Draw out every cent, of course? Each of us has such a bank. It's name is TIME. Every morning, it credits you with 86,400 seconds. Every night it writes off as lost, whatever of this you have failed to invest to a good purpose. It carries over no balance. It allows no overdraft. Each day it opens a new account for you. Each night it burns the remains of the day. If you fail to use the day's deposits, the loss is yours. There is no drawing against "tomorrow." You must live in the present on today's deposits. Invest it so as to get from it the utmost in health, happiness and success! The clock is running!! Make the most of today.

To realize the value of ONE YEAR, ask a student who failed a grade.

To realize the value of ONE MONTH, ask a mother who has given birth to a premature baby.

To realize the value of ONE WEEK, ask the editor of a weekly newspaper.

To realize the value of ONE HOUR, ask the lovers who are waiting to meet.

To realize the value of ONE MINUTE, ask a person who just missed a train.

To realize the value of ONE SECOND, ask someone who just avoided an accident.

To realize the value of ONE MILLISECOND, ask the person who won a silver medal at the Olympics.

Treasure every moment that you have! And remember time waits for no one. Yesterday is history. Tomorrow is a mystery. Today is a gift. That's why its called the present.

CHAPTER 5

LOVING

A VITAL SIGN OF, AND CRUCIAL STEP TO wholeness is to love and be loving. The words "love" and "loving" are the heart of the gospel. Love is the nature of God. It is not what He does, it is who He is. First John 4:8 states that "God is love". And John 3:16 explains that, God so loved the world that He gave His only son. In John 13:34-35, Jesus said, "A new commandment I give to you, that you love one another, as I have loved you, that you also love one another. By this all will know that you are my disciples, if you have love for one another." In yet another scripture, when Jesus was asked what was the greatest commandment, his response was quick and unequivocal, "You shall love the Lord your God with all your heart, with all your soul, with all your mind, and with all your strength.' This is the first commandment. And the second, like it, is this: 'You shall love your neighbor as yourself'. There is no other commandment greater than these" (Matthew 22:37).

It is abundantly clear that from God's vantage point, love is the greatest. It is at once the very nature of God, the identity badge that distinguishes disciples of Christ, and the first and greatest commandment. Love is the greatest! Amazingly, the world agrees! Everyone loves the word love. In one breath we can love ice cream, music, TV shows, our friends, spouse, and God. Love is a word that is over used, misused, and abused. So, let's examine what the Bible means by love.

Love Is the Greatest

The Bible is very detailed in its explanation of what love means. First Corinthians 13 is called "The love chapter" because it is totally devoted to the subject of love. It starts out by establishing the supreme import of love. Love, God's kind of love, transcends and is greater than all knowledge, faith, linguistic ability, prophetic insight, power, miracles, signs, and wonders. It is the only pure motive. Anything we do, say or achieve, regardless of how noble or altruistic, if it is not undergirded by biblical love, is useless, a complete waste of time, and will have no eternal impact. Eugene Peterson puts it succinctly in the Message Bible, "So, no matter what I say, what I believe, and what I do, I'm bankrupt without love" (1 Corinthians 13:4).

First Corinthians 13:1-3 states:

> If I could speak all the languages of earth and of angels, but didn't love others, I would only be a noisy gong or a clanging cymbal. If I had the gift of prophecy, and if I understood all of God's secret plans

and possessed all knowledge, and if I had such faith that I could move mountains, but didn't love others, I would be nothing. If I gave everything I have to the poor and even sacrificed my body, I could boast about it; but if I didn't love others, I would have gained nothing.

What this passage is saying, is that, without love, Jesus's sacrifice on the cross would have been utterly devoid of meaning or ability to save even a single soul. Think about it, if Jesus had suffered the horrendous beating that tore his back to shreds; the mockery and humiliation of the soldiers; the murderous rage of the religious leaders; the blood lust of the militant crowd; and the derision of the thief on the cross beside him; if He endured all that for any other reason or motivation than love, it would have been utterly useless, and completely impotent to save mankind. That is how critical love is! Love goes to the heart of the matter. It asks the question, "Why?" It's not what you do, but why you do it. That is what matters most. Guess who else is focused on the heart? God. First Samuel 16:7 says, "The Lord doesn't see things the way you see them. People judge by outward appearance, but the Lord looks at the heart." Biblical love is a matter of the heart.

Biblical Love

Biblical love is not a feeling. It is a choice, a decision, a commitment and an action. Biblical love is not google-eyed fantasy or day dreaming about rainbows and dew drops. It is love in working clothes, it is dirty, it is smelly, it is costly, and it is others focused. Most of all, it is practical. It does not stand by idly and make grandiose claims of affection. It is not loud, boisterous or effusive. It is not all mouth. Rather, it gives you a practical yardstick with which to measure your actions, reactions, perspectives and attitudes. It challenges your motives, encourages your perseverance and demands your allegiance.

Biblical love is not a feeling. It is a choice, a decision, a commitment, and an action.

Years ago, I was challenged by a mentor, to read 1 Corinthians 13 in an introspective way. She challenged me to locate everywhere that the word love occurred in the chapter, and to substitute my name in its place. I did and what a scathing rebuke that was! As I read and re-read the personalized chapter, I realized that, whereas I had previously felt "love", been "in love", and told friends and relatives that I loved them, my definition of love was flawed and far different from the biblical definition. First Corinthians 13:4-7 states:

> Love is patient and kind. Love is not jealous or boastful or proud or rude. It does not demand its own way. It is not irritable, and it keeps no record of being wronged. It does not rejoice about injustice but rejoices whenever the truth wins out. Love never gives up, never loses faith, is always hopeful, and endures through every circumstance.

So, if you are impatient and unkind in your treatment of people; if you are jealous or proud; if your speech is rude and laced with sarcasm; if you are demanding, self-willed, and it's your way or the highway; if you are obnoxious, bristling, brusque, and curt; and if you have a long memory of past wrongs; I don't care how you feel, you do not exhibit God's love.

I was convicted! The Holy Spirit showed me that my impatience was a manifestation of pride. I had an exalted view of myself, and did not think that I should wait on or for others. He also pointed out that my impatience made me rude and irritable. Months earlier, an acquaintance had spread a negative and untrue report about me and my family. Later, he was exposed, not only for the untruth that he told about my family, but others as well. Other character issues and flaws about him surfaced, and he was publicly humiliated. I rejoiced at my "vindication". But there and then, the Holy Spirit rebuked me. He told me that love does not rejoice in iniquity. He directed me to pray for this individual, for genuine conviction, repentance, healing, and restoration. That, is the love of God, it is a love that is beyond us and that looks out for the best interest of the other person.

Types of Love in the Bible

There are four unique types of love in the Bible. They are expressed in the Greek words – Eros, Storge, Philia, and Agape.

1. **Eros** is the Greek word for sensual or romantic love. The term originated from the mythological Greek god Eros, the god of love, sexual desire, physical attraction and physical love.

2. **Storge** is the Greek word that describes family love, the natural affection between parents and children, brothers and sisters, and so on. This is the word that describes the love Martha and Mary had for their brother Lazarus.

3. **Philia** is the Greek word that describes brotherly love. The strong emotional bond of friendship, care, respect and compassion for other people. This is the root word from which we derive the name

Philadelphia, the city of brotherly love. And, this is the love that Jesus, in John 13:35, said is the identifying mark of every disciple.

4. **Agape** is the Greek word that describes the highest form of love in the Bible. It is God's immeasurable, inexhaustible, incomparable love for human beings. "Agape love is perfect, unconditional, sacrificial and pure." (*Zavada, Jack, "4 Types of Love in the Bible."*). This word was used by Jesus when He, after His resurrection, asked Peter three times if he loved Him. Peter replied that he did, but the word he used was philia. So, Jesus asked Peter, "Do you agape me?" And Peter responds, "Yes I philia you."

Loving

Christians are created, commanded, and equipped to love. We have a tremendous God-given capacity and divine enablement to act in a loving way, regardless of how we feel. Romans 5:5 states that, "God has given us the Holy Spirit to fill our hearts with His love". So, we have the capacity to love like God loves. This capacity is deposited within us by the Holy Spirit when we receive Jesus as our savior. But we must choose to exercise or demonstrate this love.

Loving Yourself

In Matthew 22:34-40, the Bible records that a Pharisee, an expert in religious law, tried to trap Jesus with a question. He asked, "Teacher, which is the most important commandment in the law of Moses?" Jesus replied, "You must love the Lord your God with all your heart, all your soul, and all your mind. This is the first and greatest commandment. A second is equally important: "Love your neighbor as yourself".

> *People who don't love themselves,*
> *devalue and mistreat others.*

In His response, Jesus quoted the first of the ten commandments that God gave to Moses on Mount Sinai (Exodus 20). That is unquestionably, the greatest commandment. Then He added to it a second commandment from Leviticus 19:18, "Love your neighbor as yourself"; elevated this second commandment, and made it comparable to the first.

The second commandment has the premise, "as yourself". It assumes or infers that you love yourself, and then tells you to love others in the same way. Loving yourself is therefore foundational to your capacity to love others. If you do not love yourself, you cannot truly love others. This biblical truth, has been validated again and again by human experience. Hurting people, hurt people. People who don't love themselves, devalue, and mistreat others.

Loving yourself means recognizing that God is the I AM that I AM, and that His I AM image is in you. It is knowing that your identity is in Christ and Christ alone. Loving yourself means caring for your body and investing your life to make a difference. It means leaving a legacy and making every day of your life count. Loving yourself includes loving the people in your life, letting go of the past, the guilt, condemnation and mistakes, and believing God for a new beginning. It means forgiving yourself and not being tethered to fear, worry, and anxiety. Loving yourself means finding your purpose in life, and doing that thing or the things that bring you joy and deep personal satisfaction. Ladies, it means taking some "me time" to get your nails done, get a massage, buy yourself a gift, or hang out with your friends without feeling guilty about the kids. For the guys, it can be taking a day off to enjoy fishing, golf or other sport activity that you enjoy. Simply stated, loving yourself means living an abundant life, the life that Jesus came to give to us.

Often in today's society, you see two extremes. At one extreme are the people who do not love themselves. Some of these people do not even like themselves - how they look, the work they do, who they are, and so on. They do not value themselves and routinely put themselves down. Others are ashamed of themselves, their background, what they've done, and their past failures and mistakes. They sometimes falsely think that humility requires self-deprecation, and so they denigrate, discount, and devalue themselves.

Keep in mind that having a healthy dose of self-knowledge that acknowledges your quirks, recognizes your failures and mistakes, and allows you to laugh at yourself, is an important aspect of humility and being a happy and fulfilled person. But these people take it to an extreme.

Knowing yourself means discovering the core building blocks of self that make you, you.

At the other extreme are individuals who are narcissistic. The word narcissism comes from a Greek myth about Narcissus, a man who, "sees his own reflection in a pool of water and falls in love with it". Narcissists have an exaggerated view of their own importance. They think and talk often about themselves, lack empathy, and have little regard for others. They have elaborate fantasies about the future, and feel that they should have the best of everything. Narcissists feel superior to and belittle others to maintain their feeling of superiority. Despite their outward portrayal of confidence, they are grossly insecure and have a fragile self-esteem. So, they require constant praise and admiration to prop themselves up.

They have a sense of entitlement, think that others exist to serve their needs, and take advantage of others. (*Are You A Narcissist? Katherine George*).

Here again, while possessing a sense of personal importance and uniqueness are important aspects of being a happy and fulfilled person, narcissists take it to an extreme.

Knowing Yourself

Loving yourself starts with knowing yourself. Knowing yourself means understanding your temperament; strengths and weaknesses; passions and fears; desires and dreams. It means being aware of your eccentricities and idiosyncrasies; your likes and dislikes; your preferences and potential; and your tolerances and limitations. Knowing yourself means discovering the core building blocks of self that make you, you.

Why is Self-Knowledge Important?

Thales of Miletus once said, "The most difficult thing in life is to know yourself". However, good things come to those who invest in this enterprise.

1. **Confidence:** You will be happier and more confident when you can express who you are with some certainty. Also, being able to articulate and express

your dreams, desires, and goals, will help you to better achieve them.

2. **Personal Authenticity:** Knowing yourself enables you to be congruent. It allows your outward actions to correspond to or be in alignment with your inner self and core values. This supports personal authenticity and reduces internal conflict.

3. **Better Decision Making:** When you know your core values, likes, dislikes and preferred outcomes, it supports better decision making. Self-knowledge eliminates self-doubt, promotes decisive internal dialogue and provides the framework for better decision making.

4. **Self-Control:** Knowing yourself, your appetites, propensities, preferences, proclivities and bents, gives you tremendous personal insight and self-control. You become self-aware. You know how you tend to react in various situations, what motivates you, ticks you off and sets you up or off. Self-knowledge empowers you to say "no" to yourself, the devil, sin and the world. It helps you to make wise choices and say "yes" to God.

5. **Empathy and Grace:** Self-knowledge makes you less critical and judgmental of others. You are able to empathize with the failures, weaknesses and frailties

of other people. You are able to give grace and mercy to people because you can truly say with understanding, "There, but for the grace of God, go I".

6. **Empowerment:** Knowing who you are empowers you to live life to the full. It promotes self-acceptance and empowerment. You know your limitations and failures, but you also know your strengths and abilities. Knowing yourself helps you to be comfortable in your own skin. It empowers you to change what needs to change, and accept what you cannot change about yourself.

7. **Celebrate Yourself:** Self-knowledge helps you to celebrate yourself as you are. A biblically based self-assessment promotes personal approval, personal value and contentment. It helps you affirm your capabilities, own your strengths, pursue your dreams and celebrate your accomplishments.

8. **Promotes Purpose:** Knowing yourself helps you to hone in on your purpose. You don't waste time in trivial pursuits, interests or activities that do not contribute to your purpose. It helps you to identify where you belong and to minimize distractions. Knowing yourself helps you identify what is important to you, so you can focus on achieving it. It helps you prioritize and not allow people to clog your life and schedule with their interests and agenda.

The Building Blocks of Self

Knowing yourself involves discovering the core building blocks of self that make you, you. These include:

1. **Temperament**

   A lot has been written about temperaments. Dr. Tim LaHaye's book, *Spirit Controlled Temperament*, is an excellent resource on this topic. In it, he defines temperament as, "The combination of inborn traits that subconsciously affects all our behavior. These traits, which are passed on by our genes, are based on hereditary factors and arranged at the time of conception." There are four basic temperaments, the choleric, sanguine, phlegmatic, and melancholy.

   i. **Choleric** is the hot, quick, active, practical and strong willed temperament. Cholerics are driven, self-sufficient, and fiercely independent. They are self-starters, goal oriented, practical, and capable of making sound decisions. Cholerics are natural born leaders. They are quick to recognize and take advantage of opportunities, have a dogged determination, and often suc-ceed where others fail. However, Cholerics lack empathy, mercy, and compassion, and love is often not high on their list of priorities. Because Cholerics can achieve so much, they often have no sympathy for those who can't. In the Bible, apostle Paul was a choleric.

ii. **Sanguine** is the warm, buoyant, lively, and fun-loving temperament. Sanguines are extroverts and the life of the party. For them, feelings rather than reflective thoughts predominate in decision formation. The sanguine is never at a loss for words, though he or she often speaks without thinking. Sanguines are not very organized, and can readily forget appointments, responsibilities and obligations. They can be noisy, blustery, friendly, energetic, and lovable. In the Bible, apostle Peter was a Sanguine.

iii. **Phlegmatic** is the calm, cool, easygoing, and well balanced temperament. Phlegmatics have a very high boiling point and never seem to be ruffled or angry. They are very consistent and keep their emotions under control. They enjoy people, have a dry sense of humor, and are quite adept at avoiding as much involvement as possible. They are reluctant leaders, but when roused into action, they are very competent and passionate. Phlegmatics are not risktakers. They are well organized, work well under pressure, and are very dependable. Abraham was a phlegmatic.

iv. **Melancholy** is the analytical, self-sacrificing, gifted, perfectionist, with a very sensitive, emotional nature. Melancholics are introverts and can be moody. They do not make friends easily, but when made, are very loyal and faithful. They are very dependable, thorough and precise, and their exceptional analytical abilities enable them to accurately diagnose the pitfalls of any project. Melancholics tend to have high IQ, creativity and imagination. They often find their greatest meaning in life through sacrifice, and can choose a difficult life vocation, involving great personal cost. No temperament has as much natural potential when energized by the Holy Spirit as the Melancholy. Apostle John was a melancholic.

Most people are a blend of two or more temperaments, with a dominant and secondary temperament. Every temperament has strengths and weaknesses, and the Holy Spirit can work to transform the weaknesses in our temperaments. Dr. LaHaye's other book, *Transformed Temperaments*, is a biblical study of how Peter, Paul, Moses, and Abraham's temperaments were transformed and used by God.

2. Core Values
Your values are the intangible preferences you feel strongly about, that drive your actions, and that you

give great weight to in decision making. They are the moral codes and principles that form the guardrails of your life, and play a big role in your daily choices, priorities, persuading and influencing, communication, and conflict resolution. They are your non-negotiables, your internal score card. Compromising them would lead to great internal stress and conflict. For example, if family is a core value, then when you are faced with a conflict, you will make a choice that elevates family over other priorities. Your values help you to self-start, stay motivated, stay on course, be intentional, and make good choices. Your values are your personal code, internal framework, value system and worldview. It is how you determine right and wrong, and staying true to them helps you to maintain healthy self-respect and a good view of yourself.

3. Strengths and Weaknesses

Your strengths include your skills, talents, and abilities. This is the area where you are naturally equipped to excel. It also includes your character strengths like loyalty, integrity, respect, perseverance, and so on. Identifying your "strength zone", the core area where you have a convergence of skills, abilities and interests, is very important to success and fulfillment in life. Also, knowing your strength zone is one of the foundations of self-esteem, self-confidence, and security. Knowing your weaknesses is equally important. It enables you to be self-aware, realistic, and honest with yourself. Knowing your strengths and weaknesses promote confidence, humility and most of all, a balanced and healthy view of yourself.

4. Interests

To discover your interests, ask yourself the following questions. What do you like to do? What draws and holds your attention? What would you like to do for free? Interests add passion, zest and gusto to life. They provide valuable insight, not only about what you want, like or dislike, but why. It also helps to confirm your core values. Your interests can provide the road map to your future career, spouse, and so on. Working at a job that lines up with your interests will position you to succeed and give you a tremendous sense of fulfillment and wellbeing.

5. Body

Know your body constitution, shape, ability, and tolerances; what colors you like, what types of clothes look good on you, and so on. Know your biorhythms. Are you a morning person? At what time of day does your energy peak? Knowing your body helps you to maximize your potential. For example, planning activities when you are at your best ensures success, plus it respects your innate biology. "Your daily life is more pleasant when you are in sync with your biology. In every area, it is easier to enjoy life when you don't waste energy pretending to be someone you aren't" (*Know Yourself? Meg Selig Changepower*). Knowing your body includes being a good steward of your body – leading a healthy lifestyle, investing in personal grooming, learning what foods work best for your body, having regular health checkups, saying no to drugs, alcohol, and sexual immorality, and incorporating regular exercise as part of your body care regimen. Your body is a limited resource. Knowing your body helps you to maximize your body's potential.

6. Dreams

Many people are embarrassed about their dreams. They feel awkward about sharing them, because they think they are too far-fetched, or that people would laugh at them for "day dreaming". Others hide their dreams because the realities of daily life mock their dreams. However, dreams are very important in the life of a Christian, for two reasons. First, God could be, and often is the source of your dreams. If you have a strong, innate desire or dream to do something, it could be God putting that desire in your heart. The Bible states that "God is working in you, giving you the desire and power to do what pleases him" (Philippians 2:13). If you have a strong dream or desire about the future, treasure it and pray about it. God may have put that desire in your heart and He can help you fulfill it.

Secondly, your dreams give you a blueprint of the future you want, so you can partner with God to create it. In other words, your dreams provide a glimpse into your future. In my book *"Choosing a Life of Victory,* I discussed how God gave us the ability to create our world, just like He created the world. Your dreams give you the blueprint of the world, your world, that you want to create. Write down your dreams, include the details and specifics, and pray about it. The Bible says, "Write the vision; engrave it so plainly upon tablets that everyone who passes may be able to read it easily and quickly as he hastens by. This vision is for a future time. It describes the end, and it will be fulfilled. If it seems slow in coming, wait patiently, for it will surely take place. It will not be delayed" (Habakkuk 2:2-3).

Writing down your dream forces you to organize your thoughts. It helps mature your dream from wishful thinking to an executable plan. It also helps promote critical thinking about a strategy to achieve the dream. Writing your dream in detail equips you with an invaluable ability to recognize and iden-tify opportunities and individuals who will help bring your dream to reality. Also, writing down your dream gets you invested, and allows you to deploy the power of creative thinking, perseverance, and faith to bring your dream to pass. Simply stated, writing down your dream give it life!

7. Purpose

To discover your purpose, ask yourself the following questions "What are the most meaningful events of my life? What gives me joy and deep personal satisfaction? What makes me cry? Answering these questions will help you find out how you are wired, and "You may discover clues to your hidden identity, to your career, and to life satisfaction" *(Selig Changepower)*.

Knowing your core building blocks of self allows you to love yourself in the way that God intended. It frees you to be you and not have to apologize for it. Acting on that self-knowledge is liberating! It sets you free from laboring to conform to how you, or others think you "should" feel, think, or act. It promotes an internal consistency that is so critical to self-definition. It energizes and strengthens you to interface with others as the authentic you, and to genuinely love them without being needy, clingy or co-dependent. It gives you a screen with which to evaluate the people in your life and determine who belongs and who doesn't. Ultimately, it gives you the freedom to rest and nest in God!

Loving Others

Now that we have examined what it means to love ourselves, Jesus's directive to us is to "love your neighbor as yourself." Jesus then told a parable to illustrate the point.

The Parable of the Good Samaritan
(Luke 10:29-37)

The man wanted to justify his actions, so he asked Jesus, "And who is my neighbor?" Jesus replied with a story: "A Jewish man was traveling from Jerusalem down to Jericho, and he was attacked by bandits. They stripped him of his clothes, beat him up, and left him half dead beside the road. "By chance a priest came along. But when he saw the man lying there, he crossed to the other side of the road and passed him by. A Temple assistant walked over and looked at him lying there, but he also passed by on the other side.

"Then a despised Samaritan came along, and when he saw the man, he felt compassion for him. Going over to him, the Samaritan soothed his wounds with olive oil and wine and bandaged them. Then he put the man on his own donkey and took him to an inn, where he took care of him. The next day he handed the innkeeper two silver coins, telling him, 'Take care of this man. If his bill runs higher than this, I'll pay you the next time I'm here.' "Now which of these three would you say was a neighbor to the man who was attacked by bandits?" Jesus asked. The man replied, "The one who showed him mercy." Then Jesus said, "Yes, now go and do the same."

In this parable, Jesus teaches the following lessons about loving others.

1. **Love Without Bias or Prejudice**: Jesus's choice of the cast for this parable was very deliberate. At the heart of this story are ancient ethnic and religious biases and prejudices. Simply stated, the Jews hated the Samaritans. Who are the Samaritans? They are the mixed multitude, the ethnic and religious outsiders. "When the Assyrians destroyed the Northern Kingdom of Israel in 722, they exiled the upper crust of society in order to deprive the country of its leadership. At the same time, as they did elsewhere, they brought in foreign elements in order to create a mixed population unlikely to unify and revolt. These new elements eventually mixed with the native population and together they evolved a syncretistic form of Israelite worship" (*The Samaritan Schism, Lawrence H Schiffman*). These were the Samaritans.

   To love the Jewish man who had been hurt, the Samaritan had to step over centuries old biases and prejudices. Jesus said for us to "go and do the same"; meaning, this is how we should love others, without prejudice and bias.

2. **Love Without Judgement:** To the Jews listening to this parable, it was unthinkable that the despised Samaritan would be the hero of this story. This parable teaches us that love does not judge people on the basis of their ethnicity or religious

denomination. Of note, this parable was set at a time and culture when most Jews believed that if bad things happened to you, you probably deserved them, because of your sin or low living. In addition, given the Jewish religious laws and customs, if you got involved to help the injured man, you might render yourself unclean, and unfit for worship or communal life. This may have been one of the reasons why the priest and temple assistant did not want to get involved; and passed by on the other side. But the Samaritan reached out to love without judgement, and without regard to the impact on his own social status.

3. **Love Values People:** The Samaritan placed a high value on people over money, reputation, time, prejudices, religious observances, other people's opinion, and his own convenience. He loved like God! God greatly values people, and He wants us to value people too. Our love must be an expression of the value we place on others as bearing the image of God.

4. **Love Your Enemies:** Jews and Samaritans were arch enemies. The injured Jew could have been a "Samaritan-hater", and may even have personally despised and mistreated Samaritans in the past. But that is irrelevant. God does not hold us accountable for the actions or prejudices of others, but for our own. Regardless of what the injured Jew

in particular, or Jews in general, may have done to this particular Samaritan, or Samaritans generally in the past, God's love requires us to love anyway. In Matthew 5:44, Jesus said, "Love your enemies, bless those who hate you, and pray for those who persecute you".

5. **Love Compassionately**: This parable teaches us that loving others means acting in their best interest. Compassion is love in action. It means that when you see a need, you should own it and do what you can to solve it. The Samaritan did not need to hear a sermon or for God to "speak" to him to help. He saw a need, was moved with compassion, and acted to address the need. This is the pattern that Jesus laid out in the scriptures. Several scriptures record that Jesus saw a need, was "moved with compassion" and took action to meet the need – Matthew 9:36, Luke 7:12-15. We should do likewise.

6. **Love Sacrificially:** Loving others has a cost. In this parable, it cost the Samaritan money, time, attention, his own convenience, and so on. He went out of his way to care for the wounded man. He put the man on his donkey. The Jew rode and the Samaritan walked. Sometimes, loving others will take us outside our comfort zone, or cause us significant inconvenience, like it did the Samaritan.

7. **Get Others Involved to Help**: The Samaritan did all he could do, but he did not stop there. He enlisted the inn keeper to help. Sometimes, we are not in a position to help or are poorly equipped, or what we can do is limited, but we can invite and encourage others to help. The principle is, do what you can and invite others to join in.

8. **Follow Up:** The Samaritan cared enough not only to help in the moment, but to follow up later. He went over and beyond. Sometimes we are tempted to do the least we can, or to put up an appearance, or go through the motions of helping. But 1 John 3:18 challenges us to "love not in word and speech, but with actions and in truth."

Whole singles are people who love and value themselves and others in the name of the Lord. Love personifies God, so, there is no wholeness without love.

Love Languages

Just like people communicate verbally with words to be understood, love has a language. And just like speaking the English language to a person who understands only the Chinese Mandarin language will make for a very frustrating, unintelligible and bizarre "conversation", speaking love to a person in a love language that they do not understand has the exact same effect.

It is gibberish. So, for two people to effectively communicate love, it is important to find out the love language that the other person speaks, learn that language and use it to communicate your love to them.

There are 5 love languages. These were popularized in the 1992 book, *The Five Love Languages,* by Gary Chapman. Each person has a primary love language which speaks more to them than all the others. Discovering that language and speaking it regularly is the best way to say "I love you" to that individual.

1. **Words of Affirmation:** This love language entails using words to build up the other person. They could be words of appreciation for specific actions, qualities or accomplishments; or expressions of personal value, worth, affirmation and validation. These expressions can be communicated verbally or written in a card, love note, email, text and so on.

2. **Gifts**: This love language entails giving a gift. To the recipient, the gift says, "I value you" or "I was thinking about you". It also says, "you are so important to me that I took time out of my day to find this gift for you".

3. **Acts of Service**: This love language involves doing something for the other person that you know they would appreciate. It could range from getting them a cup of water, running bath water, giving

them a massage, or helping around the house. It is important that you learn what the other person likes, and not merely give them what you like or think they should like.

4. **Quality Time**: For individuals with this love language, love is spelt TIME. This involves spending time with the other person and giving them your undivided attention. Note that it is not just being there physically, while your mind is miles away. You need to be fully present, engaged, making eye contact, nodding, reflecting what you hear, actively listening and responding.

5. **Physical Touch**: This is love that is expressed through tactile contact – holding hands, touching, playful pinching, patting, massage, hugging, kissing and so on. Guys, if this is your wife's love language, it is important that you speak this language to her without a hidden agenda, and not as a prelude to sex.

Is Remarriage Biblical?

A question that I have been asked often is, "Can a Christian remarry after widowhood or divorce?" The answer is a resounding yes! I am aware that some church denominations teach that you cannot remarry after a divorce. As I shared in my personal testimony,

"My road to singleness", in the introduction and chapter 1 of this book, I grew up in a church like that, and unbeknownst to me, that legalistic thinking lurked in the recesses of my mind, only to rise to the surface after my divorce and significantly impact my attitude towards remarriage. But that thinking is not the truth. Regarding remarriage, here is what the Bible teaches:

1. **Marriage is God's Idea:** God established marriage and performed the first marriage ceremony in the garden of Eden. He created Eve and brought her to Adam (Genesis 2:18-24).

2. **Marriage is a Covenant:** It is a sacred vow and bond established before God as witness. It is not a contract to be dissolved at will or whim. Marriage should not be entered into frivolously or lightly.

3. **Marriage is a Metaphor:** Marriage is a metaphor or illustration of the relationship between Christ and the church (Ephesians 5:31-32). For the Christian, the marriage itself is a ministry, a model of Christ and the church.

4. **Marriage is Monogamous:** God's intent is that marriage is between one man and one woman for life (Mark 10:2-10, Matthew 19:6).

5. **Till Death Do Us Part:** If a spouse dies, the other spouse is free to remarry (1 Corinthians 7:39).

6. **Divorce:** God's prescription for resolving marital issues is forgiveness, healing and reconciliation. However, there are provisions for divorce in special circumstances. These include marital infidelity (Matthew 5:31-32, Matthew 1:19), abandonment (1 Corinthians 7:15), and physical abuse.

7. **No-Fault Divorce:** Outside of the above parameters, remarriage after a divorce is viewed under the law as adultery (Matthew 19:9, Luke 16:18). So also, is having an affair (Hebrews 13:4). God has a solution for adultery in the new covenant, that solution is grace, forgiveness, redemption and restoration. In John 8:1-11, when the Pharisees brought the woman caught in adultery to Jesus, He said to her, "Neither do I condemn you. Go and sin no more." Jesus absolved her.

8. **God Hates Divorce:** Divorce is very traumatic and is like an amputation. It is severely damaging to the man, woman, children and other family members involved. God hates divorce (Malachi 2:16) because of what it does to people.

9. **God Loves People More:** If a person has been divorced for any reason, the grace, mercy, and power

of God is available to heal, redeem that situation, and restore the individual. Remarriage can be a part of God's restoration plan. Joyce Meyer is a good example. So also, is Kenneth Copeland and John Osteen, the father of Joel Osteen. They remarried after a divorce and went on to fulfill the purpose of God for their lives in a successful second marriage.

10. **Marriage is Good:** Beware of individuals, denominations or doctrines that prohibit marriage or remarriage (1 Timothy 4:3). Marriage is God's idea and is good (Genesis 2:18).

11. **But Singleness is Better:** In 1 Corinthians 7:8, 32-35, the apostle Paul recommends that, whenever possible, it is better not to remarry, because an unmarried man or woman can focus on serving the Lord with single minded devotion. So, a single, celibate lifestyle of consecration is a valid biblical choice and one that is pleasing to God.

Sexuality and the Christian Single

God created sex, sexuality, and sexual desire in men and women. Psalms 139:14 states that we are fearfully and wonderfully made. However, the Bible is clear that God ordained for sex to be practiced within the confines of marriage. Contrary to the lies portrayed by

Hollywood, "Genuine love and relationship outside of marriage does not require sexual expression for fulfillment" (Fatal Attractions, Jack Hayford). Sex outside of marriage is a contravention of God's standards and can be very destructive. For a married person, sex outside of marriage is the sin of adultery, and for a single person, it is the sin of fornication. In the Bible, adultery and fornication are collectively referred to as sexual immorality.

God has very strong words against sexual immorality. In 1 Corinthians 6:18, the Bible says, "Run from sexual sin! No other sin so clearly affects the body as this one does. For sexual immorality is a sin against your own body". This scripture states categorically that sexual sin is unlike any other sin. It is in a class all by itself, because when you engage in sexual immorality, you not only sin against the Lord, and other people, but you also sin against your own body.

Sexual Sin is a Grave Sin Against the Lord

1. **Your Body Is A Temple That Houses the Holy Spirit:** First Corinthians 6:19 states, "Don't you realize that your body is the temple of the Holy Spirit, who lives in you and was given to you by God?" The Holy Spirit lives in you, so, every time you engage in sexual immorality, you are dragging the Holy Spirit, kicking and screaming and forcing Him to lay down and engage in that sexual encounter with you. You are forcing Him to fornicate or commit adultery! You

are forcing Him to have sex against His will. You are raping the Holy Spirit! You are raping God!

2. **God's Temple Is Holy, Sexual Sin Defiles and Destroys This Temple:** First Corinthians 3:16-17 states, "Don't you realize that you are the temple of God and that the Spirit of God lives in you? God will destroy anyone who destroys this temple. For God's temple is holy, and you are that temple". When you engage in sexual sin, you set yourself on a collision course with destruction. Why? Because sexual sin destroys your body. Your body is God's holy temple, and when you defile and destroy God's temple, God Himself will destroy anyone (including you), who destroys His temple.

3. **You Belong to God:** First Corinthians 7:20 states, "You do not belong to yourself, for God bought you with a high price. So you must honor God with your body." And Romans 12:1-2, instructs us to give our bodies to God and, "Let them be a living and holy sacrifice—the kind He will find acceptable. This is truly the way to worship him". In other words, sexual purity and abstinence honors God and is a living and holy sacrifice of true worship.

4. **God is Holy:** First Peter 1:14-16 states, "So you must live as God's obedient children. Don't slip back into your old ways of living to satisfy your own

desires. You didn't know any better then. But now you must be holy in everything you do, just as God who chose you is holy. For the Scriptures say, "You must be holy because I am holy." "The word translated "holy" means sacred, morally blameless, consecrated, saint" ("Be Holy for I am Holy", Aretha Grant). Habakkuk 1:13 puts it in context. It says of God, "Your eyes are too pure to look on evil and you cannot tolerate wrongdoing". This is why Jesus felt the desolate separation from His Father when He was carrying our sins on the cross. God's eyes are too pure to look on sin and wrongdoing. So, He turned His face away from His Son, when He hung on the cross gruesomely disfigured by the sins of mankind. Can you then imagine the unspeakable horror, and utter despicableness of forcing God, who lives in your body, to be, not only an onlooker, but an accomplice to and participant in sexual sin?

Why Are Sexual Sins Worse Than Other Sins?

Pastor Jack Hayford wrote an excellent book on this subject, titled "Fatal Attractions". In it, he details several reasons why sexual sins are worse than other sins, and especially destructive to the individual engaged in it.

1. Sex Sins Stain the Root of An Individual's Identity

This is the first and foundational reason why sex sins are worse than any other sin. "In the raw physiological facts of life, there is nothing so fundamental to our personhood as our genitals..... the first way in which any of us was identified was either "it's a boy" or "it's a girl"—a fact that is far more deeply related to our whole sense of who we are than most of us are willing to acknowledge." This is why there is such a "deep sense of loss and isolation that occurs when the foundation of a person's identity is violated by sexual pollution." When we first brush up against sexual immorality, it evokes something deep within us. "Notice is served from the first—before our consciences are seared through by recurrent acts—that the root of our identities has been touched in an inappropriate way, and we begin to feel a sense of loss—a shattering, a straining—as the very foundation of who we are has been shaken and violated" "An entire lifetime can be crippled, and a hopeful future can progressively disintegrate when one's identity is polluted by sexual sin" *(Hayford)*.

2. Sex Sins Exploit the Deepest Aspects of Our Emotionality

"Because sexual activity awakens our deepest passions, it also exposes us to the greatest risk of emotional violation and injury". "Since nothing is more emotionally or physically provocative than our sexuality...Sexual indulgence is deceitfully presented as a means to physically prove a person's worth (or prowess), emotionally violating those who are desperate to sense they deeply matter to other people and who yearn to feel loved" (*Hayford*).

We live in a time when sexual immorality is portrayed as the norm, infidelity is romanticized in popular music, blatant lust is falsely paraded as love, and sexual compromise is widespread. So many emotionally vulnerable women are exploited by men who disguise their warped and self-centered sexual demands as love. "If you love me, you'll do this" they say, but the woman finds out, too late, that the promised love and emotional support was all a farce. "Contrary to the bill of goods that's been sold to society, breaking every sexual convention and taboo hasn't brought any of us more liberty, only more enslavement and brokenness." Individuals who are secure in their true identity in Christ will not feel a need to prove themselves through their sexual prowess or "by allowing their personhood, values and body to be violated" *(Hayford)*.

3. **Sexual Sins Pollute the Fountainhead of Our Highest Creativity**

"Sin of all kinds---but particularly sex sins---poison us at the root of our identity, humanity and creativity." God created us in His own image, with the ultimate ability, the ability to create life, eternal life, at will.

This is the God-kind ability that separates mankind from all other creation. And this is the ability that is vandalized, abused, distorted and corrupted by sexual sin. Jesus said that the devil comes to "steal, kill and destroy". In no other area of life is this tri-fold satanic ministry more manifest and prolific than in the sexual area. When sexual immorality is given full rein, it consumes a person's time, thought and resources. The mind, creative faculties and daily activities are pre-occupied with how to find or create more opportunities for sex. This blind focus deadens the spirit, dominates the mental capacity, snuffs out any creativity and consumes all available resources. The thief is at work! These "little burglaries that we let Satan get away with ... lead to the wholesale robbery of all that matters to us." "God desires that we would see the meeting point between our spiritual and our physical capacities. If we do not learn the *discipline* of His ways in our sexual capacities (which are a part of His creative design in us), then we will never learn the *glory* of His creative capacity working through us in a spiritual dimension" *(Hayford).*

4. **Sex Sins Produce Guilt That Cripples Confidence and Authority**

"More than any other kind of sin, sexual sin produces guilt that cripples a believer's confidence and authority." "This sense of guilt and shame does not persist because the individuals do not understand

God's forgiveness; it persists because of two dynamics: first, the brutality of the adversary, and second, the vulnerability of our sexuality to unique psychological wounding." "When people surrender to sexual sin, it is common for something real to become lodged in their souls—something fixes itself in the psyche, like a monument to their failure" *(Hayford)*. They feel a crushing sense of guilt and condemnation even though they have a personal relationship with Christ, know about His love, mercy, and forgiveness; and that the Bible says that they are forgiven. They still feel the unshakeable, debilitating imprint of guilt, shame, reproach and condemnation. Sexual sin has left an invisible brand on their soul.

5. **Sex Sins Increase the Probability of Multiplying the Spread of Disease**

"The crippling shame and emotional damage of sex sins leave a permanent mark on the psyche—and often a fatal mark in the flesh of a person who has contracted a sexually transmitted disease" *(Hayford)*. HIV, herpes, gonorrhea, and many other sexually transmitted diseases have ruined lives, and destroyed their victim's hopes for marriage and having children. Nothing in life is as bitter as the regret and self-loathing of a person who knows that they are unable to marry, conceive, or raise the family that they always wanted, because of their prior sexual indiscretions. Part of the heavy weight of their self-blame come from knowing that their actions have also negatively impacted their spouse for a lifetime. Unfortunately, people are deluded into a false sense of security, either because they think that they practice "safe sex", or because they believe that there are medications available for these infections. Even though available medications may cure some of these diseases, the scar tissue or other residual issue that they leave behind often have a long term impact on the ability to conceive or raise a family.

6. Sex Sins Give Place to Appetites That Only Beget Further Immoral Behavior

When a person engages in sexual sin, like fornication, adultery, or watching pornography, a spiritual transaction takes place and he or she is corrupted by a demon of lust. This demon makes you feel justified in giving yourself the license for sexual gratification. You feel that you "deserve" sex and sexual pleasure. This sense of entitlement blurs your spiritual perception and short circuits good judgement. Essentially, your brain is now between your legs. "God's word speaks so strongly because licentiousness bypasses God's monitors on the human heart that help to establish our values.....And once given license, the spirit of lust begins its deceptive seduction". Eventually, the individual will go far beyond the bounds of what is "normal". They will develop extreme sexual appetites that "normal" sex will no longer be sufficient. Consequently, they progressively engage in more and more risky or extreme sexual behavior, looking for a "high". Often, they turn to drugs to heighten their sexual pleasure and this leads to even more bondage. "Women who dabble in sexual flirtation or use sex as a means to obtain emotional or material favors from men find themselves equally surrendered to the spirit of lust, in bondage and struggling for control" *(Hayford).* A collateral damage of this depraved, demonic, appetite for sex is the current or future spouse, who despite their best efforts, will never be able to satisfy this individual. This is why marriage does not solve this problem. The individual needs deliverance from the spirit of lust.

I strongly recommend Jack Hayford's book, *Fatal Attractions.* It covers several other reasons why sexual sins are worse than other sins and provides real life stories from Pastor Jack's counseling ministry.

Soul Ties and Spiritual Orbits

Soul Ties

A soul tie is a strong connection or bond that binds two people in the soul realm. Their two souls are "knit" together in an intense bond, such that they "cleave" to each other and become "one flesh". One of the primary ways that a soul tie is created is through sexual intimacy. God intended sex for marriage, so He included in the plan, a godly soul tie to be established during sex. This strong bond or connection draws a married couple together like magnets, they feel a special closeness, belonging, yearning, completeness, and oneness with each other. Their two souls are melded together and they feel inseparable. Ephesians 5:31 describes this process, "For this cause shall a man leave his father and mother, and shall be joined to his wife and they two shall become one flesh". This soul tie creates a bridge between their two souls. Over time, they can know each other very deeply, communicate very effectively without using words, finish each other's sentences, and become essentially an extension of each other. This is why the biblical expression for sex is "to know". The first biblical record of sex is in Genesis 4:1, "And the man knew Eve his wife; and she conceived". This deep, intimate, profound "knowing" establishes a soul tie.

A soul tie can also be formed between close friends. First Samuel 18:1 provides an example of a good soul tie between David and Jonathan. "Now when he had finished speaking to Saul, the soul of Jonathan was knit to the soul of David, and Jonathan loved him as his own soul."

Ungodly Soul Ties

When a person has sex outside of marriage, an ungodly soul tie is formed. First Corinthians 6:16 describes this process, "And don't you realize that if a man joins himself to a prostitute, he becomes one body with her? For the Scriptures say, "The two are united into one." If they have sex outside of marriage with multiple people, the multiplied soul ties further complicate the issue, and lead to tremendous vandalization and fragmentation in the soul realm. This person will have a difficult time bonding with a spouse, because they are still connected to these other people.

Also, because soul ties create a bridge between two souls, sex outside of marriage opens up demonic traffic between the two people, such that there can be a transference of evil spirits, demonic strongholds, satanic bondage, generational curses, ancestral spirits, oppressive covenants, emotional torment, and so on. Just like people can transmit physical diseases like AIDS sexually, they can also transmit soul diseases and spiritual entanglements sexually. For example, if a person has sex with another person who has the demon of lust, that unclean spirit can latch on to this other person, gain access into their lives and they too will begin to go down the path of sexual excess. If the person that they slept with has had multiple sexual partners, that also opens them up to contracting all the spiritual, emotional, and physical corruption, and pollution from all those other partners.

In addition, personal vows and other affirmations of love and commitment that people make to each other during sex or the course of an affair or other sexually involved relationship can also create a soul tie. Often in the heat of lustful passion, a couple can say to each other, "I can never feel this way about another woman or man", "I could never love another man or woman" "I will love you forever", and so on. These types of verbal commitments and covenants are essentially like marriage vows. They are intended for committed marital relationships, but when they are made within the context of sex outside of marriage, they confuse and bind the soul. When the relationship breaks up and the parties part ways, they have to go through an emotional pain and trauma that is very much like a divorce, even though they were not married.

Soul ties are the reasons why many abused women make excuses for and keep going back to the same man who had physically, verbally, and sexually abused them, doesn't love them, and treats them like dirt. It is also the reason why a guy who breaks up with a woman and doesn't want her, all of a sudden gets insanely jealous and territorial over her when she starts going out with another man. Murders without number have been committed because of soul ties.

Spiritual Orbits

When God created the world, He designed the universe with precision and order. This prefect order in the heavens controls events in the earth and produces stability and predictability. Genesis 1:14-16 states, "Then God said, "Let lights appear in the sky to separate the day from the night. Let them be for signs to mark the seasons, days, and years. Let these lights in the sky shine down on the earth." And that is what happened. God made two great lights-the larger one to govern the day, and the smaller one to govern the night. He also made the stars."

At creation, God gave the sun and moon governance or rule over the earth. The sun is the center of our solar system and the planets, including the earth orbits around it. Every day, the earth completes one full rotation on its axis, and about every 365 days, it completes one revolution or orbit around the sun. The reason why the earth and other planets orbit the sun, is because of the sun's gravitational pull. If the sun weren't there, the earth would travel in a straight line. But the gravity of the sun alters its course, causing it to travel around the sun, in a circular shape or orbit.

Just like the sun is the center of our solar system and the planets, including the earth, orbit around it, God has set in the human heart, a throne for himself. If we have Jesus the Son of God, the Sun of righteousness, as the center of our lives, and sitting on the throne of our hearts, our lives would orbit around Him, and everything will be in order. But often, we have other things or people as our center. Some people have their ministry, family, jobs or businesses at the center of their lives. If any of these is shaken, their world falls apart, and their lives spin out of control, because these people and things do not have the gravitational pull to hold their lives together, only Jesus does. Colossians 1:17 says that Christ, "Is before all things, and in Him all things hold together." As Christians, we are in Christ and our lives are supposed to revolve around Him. Acts 17:28 says that, "In Him we live and move and have our being". But when we make other people or things the center of our lives, and give them permission to sit on the throne of our hearts, or occupy the throne ourselves, the center cannot hold, and things will fall apart.

As we studied earlier, every person is a spirit, has a soul, and lives in a body. Each person's soul has its own orbit, like a planet. People we care deeply about or are in committed, long-term, covenant relationships with, such as family members, close friends and relatives are in or share our spiritual orbits. When people are in your spiritual orbit, they have a unique connection with you, and have access to your soul realm. Your orbits intersect, such that they can "sense" when something is going on with you. They tend to call, "just at the right time" or you were just thinking about them, and they show up or you run into them, and so on. For a married couple, family members and close godly friends, being in each other's spiritual orbit is a blessing. They can accurately "sense" things about the other person, or "feel" a need to pray for them, or simply "know" that something is wrong, even when they are thousands of miles apart. This connection helps them to support, cover, and encourage one another.

Spiritual Orbits and Sexual Sin

However, when a person has sex outside of marriage, they open the door and let their sexual partner into their spiritual orbit. This is because the sex act involves a very deep level of "knowing", soul interlocking, physical intimacy, vulnerability, and bonding. This soul tie creates a bridge between their two souls and lets their sexual partner into their orbit. Same thing can happen when you have close friends and confidants who are not believers in Christ. These deep connections where you, "bare your soul" to another person can establish a strong bond in the soul realm. Have you ever wondered why, when you finally make up your mind to become serious with God and grow in your relationship with Him, you "just happen" to get a call from your former unsaved boyfriend? Or why, when you are in a vulnerable state emotionally, you just happen to "run into" that girl or guy that you slept with years ago and he or she talks you into having sex again? Or why you just happen to meet a person "by chance" who becomes a big negative influence in your life for evil? Or why you keep feeling this strong gravitational pull to a person, place or activity that you know is toxic for you? It's a set up by the devil! He will try to tell you that these incidents are "a sign" that "it was meant to be" or that you are supposed to be with these people, but that is a lie. The truth is that you opened yourself up, through unholy connections, and granted access to the wrong people, so that your orbit attracts or intersects with these people who are agents of the devil, with an assignment from hell to destroy your life.

Here's the sum, when you are living in sexual sin, your life is out of order and in rebellion against Christ. Your sexual sin and fleshly desire is your idol, because you elevate it above, listen to, and obey its command instead of God's. Also, you make your sexual partner your idol, because you place their desires and voice above that of the Lord. In so doing, you give them permission to occupy the throne meant for God in your life and they are in the center of your spiritual orbit. Unfortunately, despite their promises, they cannot hold things together, only Christ can. So, your life will spin out of control until you dethrone them, say no to sexual sin, and allow Jesus to ascend the throne of your heart. When this inner coronation takes place, Jesus becomes your center, and in Him all things hold together, so nothing that comes your way will cause you to spin out of orbit.

Sexual Images

A powerful token of sexual sin, and the soul ties that it engenders, is the associated images. Sexual sin generates passionate images that linger and evoke strong emotions. Whether they are images from actual sexual encounters, or pornographic images, these images appear to be branded in the mind, and become strong chains that bind and hold the individual captive. Often, even after the individual has decided to walk away from the sin of sexual immorality, they cannot get rid of the images, and at the opportune moment, the devil energizes those images, empowers them, and use them to bring the person down. These attacks are especially vicious, intense and swift. A person who has repented from sexual sin, can have sudden, overpowering, flashback images of the sexual act with a person that they felt especially close to, or had a "special" connection with, or had a sexual relationship with over a long period of time. These attacks are swift and effective; the image is suddenly introduced into the mind, backed by very strong emotions, and before you know it, it hijacks the thought process, and moves your will to commit a sexual sin. The pressure is intense, and these images become the access points, or tokens for the demon of lust to re-enter, re-take possession, and take the person down. These attacks leave the individual feeling powerless and defeated. The shame, repeated failure, and feeling of helplessness to break free, drive the individual to depression, hopelessness, despondency and despair. Many feel trapped, and some consider suicide.

How to Break Soul Ties and Terminate Spiritual Orbit Access

1. **Stop:** Stop crying to God to save you. He already has done His part; the next move is yours. You made wrong choices that led you into sexual bondage. You can make biblical choices to take you out, starting now.

2. **Repent**: Confess your sexual sin(s) and genuinely repent before God.

3. **Forgive:** Forgive the other person if you have any lingering issues or offense.

4. **Destroy Any Tokens:** Any tokens such as gifts, rings, flowers, love letters, photos, and so on, given or received in connection with the sexual relationship should be destroyed.

5. **Uproot Root of Bitterness:** In Hebrews 12:15, the Bible warns that any root of bitterness will bring corruption and defilement into your life. So, uproot any bitterness in your heart, and lay it before the Lord.

6. **Cancel Every Vow:** Any personal vows or verbal commitments that supported or helped form the soul tie should be renounced and revoked. Since they were enacted verbally, you can undo and cancel them verbally.

7. **Renounce and Revoke the Soul Tie:** Declare, "In Jesus name, I renounce and revoke every soul tie formed between me and _____ as a result of our sexual sin. Jesus has forgiven me and set me free. I declare and walk in my freedom in Christ.

8. **Break the Soul Tie:** Exercise your authority in Christ to sever the soul tie. Declare, "In Jesus name, I now break, dismantle, and sever any ungodly soul ties formed between me and_____. I declare it to be null, void, and of no effect. Jesus has set me free, and whom the Son sets free is free indeed.

9. **Terminate Spiritual Orbit Access:** Exercise your authority in Christ to shut the door that you opened to the wrong people to access your orbit. Declare, "In Jesus name, _____, I shut you out of my soul realm. I unplug myself from you, and terminate your access into my spiritual orbit. I declare that Jesus is enthroned in my heart, is at the center of my life, and the gate keeper to my orbit.

10. **Cast Down the Images:** Second Corinthians 10:4 states that we have power, through God to cast down imaginations. So, when sexual memories and images surface in your mind, speak up, and rebuke them in the name of Jesus. Dismantle and cast them down. Do not allow them to linger. Declare that your imagination is flooded with the light of God (Ephesians 1:18).

11. **Bind the Strongman:** Bind the strongman spirit of whoredoms, and the strongman perverse, seducing, and lying spirits, and cast them out of your life (Matthew 12:29). Loose the Holy Spirit, the spirit of holiness, purity, and truth

12. **Bind the Demons:** Bind the evil spirits sent by the devil and his strongmen to supervise and enforce the sexual sin, bondage and soul-ties in your life. Terminate their assignment, shut down their operation, and cast them out.

13. **Appropriate the Blood of Jesus:** Declare, "The blood of Jesus purchased my salvation and deliverance. All my sins, including my sexual sins were paid for in full. There is no condemnation for me because I am in Christ, so I reject every voice that speaks against me in judgement and condemnation. Thank you, Lord, that the blood of Jesus is

speaking over me, freedom, deliverance, victory, strength, favor, and grace."

14. **Take Communion:** Take communion to declare your union with Christ and deliverance from the devil and his kingdom (Colossians 1:13).

How Can I Be Sexually Pure?

When Jesus acquitted and absolved the woman caught in adultery, He said to her, "go and sin no more" (John 8:10-11). It is of critical importance that after being delivered from ungodly soul ties, spiritual orbits, and other sexual bondage, that you maintain sexual purity. Jesus warned that when an unclean spirit is cast out of a person, it goes around, looking for an alternate place to reside, and finding none, it will recruit seven other spirits more evil than itself, and return to the "house" or person from whom it was cast out, to re-occupy that life; so, that person's end-state is worse than before they were delivered (Luke 11:24-26, Matthew 12:43-45). This is why it is crucial to maintain sexual purity going forward. Here's how:

1. **Believe That Sexual Purity is Possible and You Have the Power:** To be sexually pure, you must believe that sexual purity is possible, and that you are well able, through Christ, to live a pure life.

Despite the lies that the depraved culture, media, and the devil is propagating, not "everybody is doing it". On the contrary, there is an army of single Christian men and women who are living a genuinely celibate lifestyle that honors the Lord. I am one of them. To the glory of God, I have been celibate for over 10 years, and pure in mind and body. It is one of the most powerful testimonies of my life, to be able to look my children in the eye, and affirm to them, that I have honored the Lord in my sexuality. You can too! All you need to do, is to make different choices. Following are the principles that have helped me and countless others to live sexually pure in a corrupt and polluted world. These principles will work for you, if you, with the help of the Holy Spirit, apply them to your life.

2. **The First Place to Start Is in the Mind**: Sexual purity begins with your thoughts. You must set aside what you think about sex outside of marriage and agree with God that it is a terrible sin. You must see, think, believe, and feel about it, the way God does. Sex outside of marriage is not okay, it is not exciting, it is not the cultural norm, it is not fun, it is not a mistake, it is not a "small thing". It is a sin and an egregious breach against a Holy and righteous God.

3. **You Must See Your Body as Physically a Part of Christ**: This makes your engagement in sexual sin

a gross violation of the Lord himself. It makes it tantamount to raping Christ. The Bible says, "Don't you realize that your bodies are actually parts of Christ? Should a man take his body, which is part of Christ, and join it to a prostitute?" The emphatic answer comes back, "Never!" (1 Corinthians 6:15). That should be your feelings exactly! Whenever confronted with the choice to engage in sexual sin, your response should always be an emphatic, "Never!".

4. **Don't Excuse or Justify Sexual Sin:** Tear down the wrong reasoning, thought process and self-talk that justifies and excuses the sin of sexual immorality. This is the thought process that says, "I can do anything I want. I am not hurting anybody." First Corinthians 6:12 confronts this argument head on and exposes the lie. It states, "You say, "I am allowed to do anything"—but not everything is good for you. And even though "I am allowed to do anything," I must not become a slave to anything." Nothing is so, "not good for you" and enslaves so quickly and completely as sexual sin. The crushing feelings of guilt, condemnation, worthlessness, personal loathing, erosion of the sense of self, personal dignity, and value that follow is massive and debilitating. Not to mention the waves of emptiness and craving that drive the person back again and again for more, until they are on the brink of hopelessness and despair.

As overseer of the prayer ministries at our church, I have counseled so many people trapped in sexual sin. The stories and the resulting devastation are always the same. Sexual sin promises excitement and fulfillment, but it ends up leaving people in a dark, deep, pit; ashamed, estranged from God, hating themselves, and sorely afraid. The behavior that once provided illicit pleasure now leaves them scarred, and branded with an invisible brand on their soul.

I also served in a ministry that called first time guests who visited our church and requested prayer. I will never forget one woman I called. As soon as I identified who I was, she began to weep; deep, heaving sobs. I held the phone, waited, and prayed. I thought she had just lost a family member. Eventually she quieted down enough to tell me what happened. She was a single Christian woman who had been living for God. That day, she gave in to temptation and had sex. She was an absolute wreck! That sin violated and wounded her so deeply. Whatever temporary pleasure she had experienced was totally eclipsed by the torrent of shame, guilt, and brokenness she felt. I think back to that woman often. For her, and so many others whom I have counseled, it was not worth it, not in the least.

5. **You Must Tear Down the Wrong Reasoning**: Tear down the thought process and self-talk that justifies sexual sin as fulfilling a legitimate need. This is the lie that says, sex is a natural need just like

food. I need sex, just like I need food. God made me a sexual being, so my craving for sex outside of marriage is a legitimate natural need, and so, I can and should satisfy my sexual cravings. First Corinthians 6:13-14 addresses and challenges this lie. "You say, "Food was made for the stomach, and the stomach for food." But you can't say that our bodies were made for sexual immorality. They were made for the Lord, and the Lord cares about our bodies." God made both our stomachs and our sexual parts. And here the Bible states emphatically that the comparison is false. Yes, food was made for the stomach and the stomach for food, but our bodies were not made for sexual immorality. Our bodies were made for the Lord, and sex outside of marriage violates that purpose, pollutes our soul, and corrupts and destroys the body. God created our bodies and He created sex. He has told us plainly that the only proper exercise of our sexual appetites is within marriage.

6. **Make a Personal Commitment to Sexual Purity**: Dedicate your sexual parts to God as instruments of righteousness and ask Him for grace and help to live sexually pure. Romans 6:12-13 states, "Do not let sin control the way you live; do not give in to sinful desires. Do not let any part of your body become an instrument of evil to serve sin. Neither present your body parts to sin as instruments of unrighteousness; but present yourselves to God, as alive from

the dead and your body parts as instruments of righteousness unto God'" This scripture directs us to be intentional and to take decisive action to dedicate our sexuality and sexual parts completely to God, to honor and glorify Him. This is exactly what Joseph did. He had made a commitment to God to be sexually pure. So, when Potiphar's wife accosted and tried to seduce him, his mind was already made up and his response was clear, "How could I do such a wicked thing? It would be a great sin against God" (Genesis 39:9). The lesson is clear. Decide now what your convictions are about sexual sin, and determine in advance what your response will be when tempted to engage in sexual immorality. If you wait until you are facing temptation, to begin to debate in your mind what you should do, it will be too late, you will be overwhelmed.

7. **Guard the Gateways to Your Mind and Your Imagination**: Guard your eye gate, your ear gate and your mouth gate. Shut the door on anything that pollutes your mind sexually. Jesus taught that no one commits sexual sin physically who has not already done so mentally and emotionally (Matthew 5:28). So, the place to stop sexual immorality, is to stop it from dominating the thoughts and growing into lust. James 1:14-15 describes the progression: "Temptation comes from our own desires, which entice us and drag us away. These desires give birth

to sinful actions. And when sin is allowed to grow, it gives birth to death".

What this means practically, is that you guard what you expose yourself to through the television, music, radio, magazines, and so on. Take authority over your eyes! You simply cannot feed your mind sexually explicit material when you are seeking to live pure. When the movie "Wolf of Wall Street" came out, I went to see it. Unfortunately, I had relied on someone else's recommendation and did not do my own research. I was told that it was a good movie, so I decided to go and see it. Well, I had to get up and walk out during the movie, due to the sexually explicit material. I could not sit there and consume that filth and expect my mind to be sexually pure. Why torture yourself? Why expose yourself to impure material and then struggle to stay pure? I understand that there is so much sexual content everywhere and it is hard to find clean material. However, a firm commitment to sexual purity requires that you invest the time and resources to identify leisure activities, and viewing material that is clean. For me, what that means is that for relaxation, when I am not watching the Christian channels, I watch old movies, westerns, and sitcoms. I find that even though they are not "Christian", they were produced at a time when "wholesome family values" coincided more with Judeo Christian values, and so they tend to have moral themes and outcomes, and little, if any, sexual content. For more modern clean movies, I sometimes watch the Hallmark channels. Also, there are many Christian movies available through Christian TV channels or on-line. One note of caution. A side effect of watching old sitcoms and westerns, is that they tend to be overloaded with commercials advertising medicines for the elderly. I mute or skip them, so I don't have that junk lodged in my mind either.

8. **Fill Your Mind and Heart with the Word of God:** If you fill your mind with the word of God, then there is no room for impure thoughts and images. Daily study and ongoing meditation on the word of God, talking to God throughout the day, regular church attendance, listening to Christian programming on TV, playing worship music, and serving others, will saturate your mind with the Word. Psalm 119:9 puts it succinctly, "How can a young person stay pure? By obeying your word." This applies equally to older people as well. Psalm 119:11 echoes the same theme, "I have hidden your word in my heart that I might not sin against you." And 1 Thessalonians 4:3 makes it crystal clear that our sexual purity is God's will. So many singles ask, "what is God's will for my life?" Here it is, in black and white. "For this is the will of God, your sanctification, that you abstain from sexual immorality". It doesn't get clearer than this.

9. **Identify Your Triggers:** At the beginning of this chapter, we discussed the critical import of self-knowledge, and how knowing yourself can help you identify your personal triggers – your appetites, proclivities, weaknesses, and what sets you up or off. Every individual has triggers. These are internal thresholds, barriers or mechanisms that when breached or compromised, can precipitate a wrongful choice. Knowing these triggers and guarding against them is a critical piece of your armor in winning the battle against sexual immorality. Emotional vulnerability can set you up for moral failure. Also, "unmet physical needs can predispose a person to thinking thoughts, speaking words and making choices that open the door to the devil". In my book, *Choosing a Life of Victory,* I discussed four states of mind that predispose people to make poor choices. This is memorialized in the acronym HALT, which stands for hungry, angry, lonely, and tired. Do not allow yourself to get too hungry, angry, lonely, and tired. Resolve these situations quickly, and before making any foolish choices. If your trigger is a magazine, a place, a song, and so on, make a personal commitment, and work with your accountability partner to develop mechanisms to guard against your exposure to these triggers. If you watch porn on the internet, then installing electronic barriers, passcodes that you don't have access to, or software that alerts

your friends and family if you wander into danger territory, can provide needed protection. Knowing your personal triggers is great, but your freedom comes when you take personal responsibility to act, based upon that knowledge.

10.   Pray and Proclaim Your Identity in Christ: Your most potent protection against the lure and chain of sexual sin, is knowing who you are in Christ, believing what God says about you, and declaring your identity in Christ. Seeing yourself as the righteousness of God will keep you from wallowing in the slime pit of sexual sin. Knowing that you have the mind of Christ, and are a partaker of His divine nature, empowers you to act in keeping with the truth of who you are. To illustrate, a sheep may fall into the mire, but it knows that it does not belong there and would get out as quickly as possible, shake the mud off, and trot off as fast as it can go. But a pig is a different story, it will wallow in the mud and mire, because that is its natural habitat. This is why the devil works so hard to convince people trapped in sexual sin that it is not only what they do, but that it is who they are, because if they can believe the lie that they are filthy pigs, then they will stop fighting and lay down in the mud. Declaring who you are in Christ empowers you to say NO to sexual temptation. Knowing that sin no longer has dominion over you, enables you to exercise your authority as a son or daughter of God to live or break free from sexual sin. Praying in that authority and power shuts down the devil's operation, and terminates the destructive assignment of sexual sin in your life.

11. **You Are Not Powerless:** This is the biggest lie of the devil, and his ultimate theft, the theft of your authority in Christ. When a person is trapped in sexual addiction, the devil's supreme tactic is to intimidate them into submission. He works to convince them that the odds are so much against them, that they don't even try to engage the enemy. But the devil is a liar! The truth of God is that you are not powerless against the enemy and his wiles. Nor are you powerless against the bullying and overpowering pressure of your flesh. There is power, in the name of Jesus to break every yoke. That moment that feels so hopeless, when you have fallen again into sexual sin, for what seems like the millionth time after you've promised yourself, and God, that you will never do it again, that moment, is often when you are closest to your breakthrough. Do not give up! Stand still and see the salvation of the Lord, for the addiction you see today, you shall see it again, no more, forever, for the Lord will fight for you" (Exodus 14:14). It is important to note that the struggle itself, is not evidence of failure, rather, it is evidence of the power of the Holy Spirit working inside you to set you free. As long as you keep crawling back

up, and speaking the word of God, regardless of how defeated, battered, weary, and worn you feel, you will break free from sexual bondage.

Can A Christian Single Use Sexual Toys?

Sometimes, the question is asked whether a Christian single can use sexual toys. My answer is the same as for sexual immorality. Why torture yourself? Why expose yourself to sexual emotions, imaginations and simulations, and then struggle to stay pure? It simply is not worth it! Proverbs 6:27 asks the same questions, "Can a man (or woman) scoop a flame into his lap and not have his clothes catch on fire? Can he walk on hot coals and not blister his feet? Using sexual toys is doing exactly that, plus it is doing what James 1:14-15 says not to do. It is stoking the fires of your sexual desire and fanning it into a roaring flame. This is an unwise enterprise, particularly given the fact that, as a single person, you do not have biblically approved avenues to satisfy those desires in a God-honoring way. So, for a single Christian, using sexual toys is an investment in sinful thoughts and actions. It will only open the door to lust, temptation and sin. Galatians 6:7 warns, "Do not be deceived, God is not mocked, for whatever a man sows, that he will also reap. For he who sows to the flesh will of the flesh reap corruption, but he who sows to the Spirit will of the Spirit reap everlasting life".

Jesus in His teachings made it clear that God weighs both our thoughts and actions. He repeatedly made the point that you must say no to temptation, not only physically, but mentally, emotionally, and in your imagination. In Matthew 5:21-30, Jesus taught that sinful actions like murder and adultery begin in the heart and imagination. I heard Dr. Alicia Chole, once say, "Don't live out in your thoughts what you can't live out in your life." That is a truth to live by in every area of life, but particularly in the sexual area. Using sexual toys and indulging in sexual simulations as a Christian single is flirting with sexual sin, which is the direct opposite of what God says to do. He says to flee sexual immorality (1 Corinthians 6:18). We have already studied 1 Thessalonians 4:3 which clearly states that God's will is for us to "abstain from sexual immorality". The pathway of life is littered with the wreckage of Christians who thought they could flout this clear scriptural directive, ignore the express will of God and somehow emerge unscathed. Do not be one of them.

Biblical Dating

Dating is a modern concept. It did not exist in biblical times. The word is not even in the bible. In the culture of Jesus's day, it was not proper for couples to be seen together in public until after they are officially betrothed. However, the fact that the word "dating" is not in the Bible, does not mean that we are left to our own devices to initiate, and pursue relationships on our own, or the world's terms. "Though the Bible doesn't talk directly about dating, it does speak volumes about relationships, godly interactions, and principles that can be applied to how you date" (What Does The Bible Actually Say About Dating? Fileta). The Bible provides clear guidelines on Christian dating – who to date, how to date, dating dos and don'ts, and so on. But first, let's define biblical dating.

The Biblical Model

The Bible states in Ephesians 5:31-32 that godly marriage between a man and woman is an illustration of the relationship between Christ and the church. So, while the Bible does not have specific dictates about dating, we can look to the picture of Jesus and the church, to discern a right approach to initiating and pursuing a godly pre-marital relationship.

The Bible is one big love story. The story begins with a father wanting a bride for His Son. The Son comes to earth, chooses His bride, initiates the relationship, pursues her, woos her, draws her to Himself, wins her heart, and betrothed's her to Himself, and when the bride was uncovered, compromised, entangled, and vulnerable, He gave himself to save and redeem her. She owed a terrible sin debt that she could not pay, and He gave His life to pay her sin debt in full. She in turn responds to His loving overtures with whole-hearted devotion, and a gesture of adoration that says, I love you Lord!

This is the model that Christian dating should emulate and reflect. With that context in mind, let's examine the current widespread model of modern dating and contrast that with the biblical model. In my research for this book, I found precious little material on biblical dating. However, I came across an excellent article from Focus on the Family (Biblical Dating, Croft), that discussed biblical dating concepts, definitions, and practices.

Biblical Dating

Is a "method of introduction and carrying out of a pre-marital relationship between a single man and a single woman:

1. That begins (maybe) with the man approaching and going through the woman's father or family", where applicable, to initiate the relationship;

2. That is conducted under the authority and oversight of the woman's father, family, church, spiritual mentor, elder, leader or accountability partner.

3. "That always has marriage, or at least a determination regarding marriage to a specific person as its direct goal."

Modern Dating

"Is a method of introduction and carrying out of a pre-marital relationship between a single man and a single woman that:

1. Begins with either the man or the woman initiating" the relationship directly with the other person;

2. Is conducted outside the oversight or authority of either person's family, church, authority figure or accountability partner

3. "That may or may not have marriage as its goal and is often purely "recreational" or "educational".

This outline of biblical dating lines up very well with the model of Christ and the church. Note that in biblical dating, a Christian man may initiate directly with a Christian woman as Jesus Christ so often initiates directly with us. This is also a practical reality, because many single Christian women, don't have a father or father figure involved in their lives, or anyone who is able, or willing to play the role of go-between during the initiation of the dating relationship.

Elements of Biblical Dating

There are four key elements of biblical dating:

1. **Mindset:** The biblical model requires a made up mind. It requires a firm conviction and commitment by both parties to honor God, put Christ at the center, and bring their dating relationship under His authority and Lordship.

2. **Oversight:** Under the biblical model, the initiation and subsequent dating relationship should be under some oversight and supervision. That oversight role can be filled by the man or woman's pastor, family members, godly mentors, and accountability partners who love the couple and are committed to seeing God's plan and purpose established in their lives.

3. **Transparency:** For biblical dating, it is important that the couple plan their dates in a public place, and/or in group activities with other individuals who know and support them.

4. **Marriage Focused:** Maybe the biggest distinction between biblical dating and worldly dating is that the relationship must have as its clear goal, the evaluation of marriage by both parties.

These four elements of biblical dating bring tremendous structure and definition to the dating relationship; provides safeguards for the couple; and protection from sexual sin and temptation. When they submit their dating relationship to the authority and Lordship of Jesus Christ; and the sunshine and warmth of godly oversight and accountability; they shield themselves from the temptations and lures that secrecy and undue privacy can produce. Also, keeping marriage as the main goal clarifies and disciplines the relationship. Today, people engage in "dating" who have no intention or goal of being married in the short or long term. Sadly, in many such situations, "dating" is only a code word for "sleeping with". I believe that if you cannot see yourself getting married in a year or two, you probably should not be dating.

Differences Between Modern Dating and Biblical Dating

In his article, Scott outlines the following differences between Biblical dating and modern dating:

1. "Modern dating philosophy assumes that there will be several intimate romantic relationships in a person's life before marriage. In fact, it advocates "playing the field" in order to determine "what one wants" in a mate. Biblical dating has as its goal to be emotionally and physically intimate with only one member of the opposite sex... your spouse.

2. Modern dating tends to be egalitarian. (No differences between men and women in spiritual or

emotional "wiring" or God given roles.) Biblical dating tends to be complementarian. (God has created men and women differently and has ordained each of these spiritual equals to play different and valuable roles in the church and the family).

3. Modern dating tends to assume that you will spend a great deal of time together (most of it alone). Biblical dating tends to encourage time spent in group activities or with other people the couple knows well.

4. Modern dating tends to assume that you need to get to know a person more deeply than anyone else in the world to figure out whether you should be with him or her. The biblical approach suggests that real commitment to the other person should precede such a high level of intimacy.

5. Modern dating tends to assume that a good relationship will "meet all my needs and desires," and a bad one won't--- it's essentially a self-centered approach. Biblical dating approaches relationships from a completely different perspective --- one of ministry and service and bringing glory to God.

6. Modern dating tends to assume that there will be a high-level of emotional involvement in a dating relationship and some level of physical involvement as well. Biblical dating assumes no physical

intimacy and more limited emotional intimacy out-side of marriage.

7. Modern dating assumes that what I do and who I date as an adult is entirely up to me and is private (my family or the church has no formal or prac-tical authority). Biblical dating assumes a context of spiritual accountability, as is true in every other area of the Christian life" *(Croft)*.

In summary

1. "Modern dating seems to be about *"finding"* the right person for me while biblical dating is more about "*being*" the right person to serve my future spouse's needs and be a God glorifying husband or wife.

2. In modern dating, intimacy precedes commitment. In biblical dating commitment precedes intimacy.

3. The modern dating approach tells us that the way to figure out whether I want to marry someone is to act like we are married. If we like it, we make it official. If we don't, then we go through something emotion-ally -- and probably physically -- like a divorce. In biblical dating, Scripture guides us as to how to find a mate and marry, and the Bible teaches, among other things, that we should act in such a way so

as not to imply a marriage level commitment until that commitment exists before the Lord." *(Croft)*.

4. Biblical dating is akin to courtship; which is the practice of establishing an intense pre-marital relationship, with the desire to see if marriage is the right choice for the couple; whereas dating is often more of a social event whereby two people meet for companionship.

Preparation for Dating

Preparation is important to ensure a successful dating relationship that honors God, and achieves biblical objectives. Here are some steps:

1. **Establish Your Parameters:** Ask yourself the following questions, what am I looking for in marriage? What do I want in a mate and why? What kind of marriage would I like to have? What are my bible-based non-negotiables to ensure the type of marriage I want? What are my beliefs and convictions about dating and marriage?

2. **Evaluate Yourself:** Ask yourself the question, am I the kind of man/woman that would attract the type of person I want? How can I become the right person? Am I prepared to put in the work to become

262

the person I need to be, in order to achieve and maintain the type of home and marriage that I want?

3. **Reflect on Your Personal Relationship with Christ:** Are you a born again Christian? If yes, are you growing and maturing in your relationship with Christ? If you aspire to be a godly husband or wife, what have you done, or plan to do, to prepare for that role?

4. **Assess Your Readiness:** Are you at a place in your life where you are ready and able to marry? Keep in mind that dating is for the purpose of marriage. Scott recommends, "In my view, if you can't happily picture yourself married within a year, you're not in a position to date" *(Croft)*. I would extend the dating timeframe to one to two years.

5. **Pray:** If you have a desire to be married, believe that God has a spouse for you, (Genesis 2:18) and ask God for your spouse (Proverbs 19:14). Then, trust that God will give you the right person in line with His and your heart's desire (Psalms 37:4). Determine that you will not settle for less than God's best for you.

6. **Establish a Standard:** Look to the Bible to decide on the kind of person to date. Since the goal of biblical dating is marriage, you should not date anyone

you cannot marry. So, do not evaluate dating prospects based solely on chemistry or attraction, but based on the criteria in the word of God. The bible provides specific guidelines:

a. Christians must date only Christians. Second Timothy 2:22 (TLB)

b. Do not date a non-believer (2 Corinthians 6:14-15, James 4:4 and Amos 3:3).

c. Don't date a person who professes to be a Christian but acts contrary to the word of God (2 Corinthians 5:11).

d. Don't date a person with a bad temper – (Proverbs 22:24).

e. Don't date a lazy person (2 Thessalonians 3:6, 10).

f. Don't date a person just because of their looks – (1 Peter 3:4).

g. Don't date a person just because of money (1 Timothy 6:6-10).

h. Date someone with a good attitude (Proverbs 17:22).

i.   Don't be selfish or date a selfish person (Philippians 2:4).

j.   Date someone who is positive and supportive (Philippians 2:1-2).

k.   Let the relationship grow step by step (2 Peter 1:5-7).

7. **Clarify the Roles:** Men should initiate, and women respond. The man should initiate asking the woman out. This is important because, "single men need to learn how to lead, and single women need to learn to let a man assume spiritual leadership in the relationship" (*Croft*). The Bible states in 1 Corinthians 11:3, that the man is the head in the home. The dating relationship is a great place to start this role clarity.

8. **Establish Accountability Partners or Mentors:** It could be a married couple that you know and respect, and that loves and care for you both. Even if you don't establish a formal accountability structure, at least ensure that the two of you begin to meet in public with others who know one or both of you well, so that there will be consistent accountability, as well as an outside perspective and support for your dating relationship.

9. **Be Intentional:** Clarify the intent of the relationship from the outset. The man should take the lead to define what his intent is in pursuing this relationship. Doing this provides protection and covering for the woman.

10. **Establish Boundaries:** Discuss upfront to determine and establish boundaries for your dating relationship. Agree at the outset that you will not engage in sex, or physical contact that could lead to sex. Decide where to draw the line, and agree that you will support each other in enforcing that boundary.

What to Do/Not Do on Dates

a. Don't participate in the darkness of wild parties and drunkenness, or in sexual promiscuity and immoral living, or in quarreling and jealousy – Romans 13:13.

b. Don't have sex during dating – 1 Corinthians 6:13

c. Treat single women as sisters and single men as brothers - 1 Timothy 5:1-2

If You Have Already Sinned Sexually

1. Stop.

2. Acknowledge your sin and confess it to God (Psalms 32:5).

3. Ask God to forgive you (1 John 1:9).

4. Receive Christ's forgiveness and reject the guilt and condemnation from the devil (Romans 8:1-2).

5. Sin no more – genuinely repent and commit to celibacy (John 8:10-11, 1 Corinthians 6:10-11).

6. Break the soul tie and other bondage established by the sexual sin.

Is Online Dating Biblical?

It depends on the role or purpose that the online dating platform serves. If the online platform is merely a meeting point where the man and woman meet, much like they would meet at a church, grocery store, or other open forum, that is okay, provided that they then transition the actual dating relationship to the biblical model described above. However, if the online dating platform becomes the medium for the ongoing relationship, and they do not submit their dating to the biblical model and guidelines discussed above, then it is not biblical. The point is that whether the man and woman meet each other at a school, church, or online dating platform, is not what determines whether their dating is biblical. Once they meet and decide to date, they should then submit their dating relationship to the biblical model outlined above and modeled by Christ.

The real challenge with online dating is that those platforms can become the haunt of predators, sex offenders, and people who use the cloak of anonymity that it provides to deceive and beguile. Unlike meeting someone at a church or school, where you can more readily and accurately validate their personal profile, online dating platforms are rife with misrepresentations. Most people don't even use their real names online, plus they make false claims, and use false photos, or photos that are decades old. Also, there have been several news reports about women being date raped or murdered by men they met online. So, you must exercise extreme caution with online dating.

Social Media and the Quest for Love

We live in a social media world; a world that has heightened, exploited, and exposed our vulnerabilities. One major area of vulnerability that has been elevated by, and paraded on social media, is the hunger for love, acceptance, and identity. God created us with a fundamental need for love, friendship, companionship, and intimacy. However, He intended for this need to be filled through healthy relationships with our family, friends, spouse, and so on; and not by a horde of internet "friends"; who really don't know, and don't care about us. Today, people measure their worth by how many likes they get on social media, and who is following them. Individuals who have no meaningful contribution to society, have become a social media "personality", "influencer" or "celebrity." Social media has spawned a selfie generation, people who are obsessed with themselves, and love to put themselves on display. This self-absorption, coupled with the hunger for validation by people, has led to tragic consequences! Vulnerable people, desperately looking for acceptance and love, have been crushed, publicly humiliated, and driven to suicide by viscous, public attacks, and ridicule on social media.

In Genesis 29, the Bible tells the story of one woman's desperate search for love and acceptance. This is the story of Leah. Jacob did not love Leah, and was tricked into marrying her. Leah felt unwanted and unloved. She expressed her desperate search for her husband's love in the names she gave her children. She named her first born son Reuben, which means, "behold, a son"; for she said, "The Lord has noticed my misery, and now my husband will love me". When she had her second son, she named him Simeon, which means, "he has heard"; for she said, "The Lord has heard that I was unloved and has given me another son". Then she had a third son, and named him Levi, which means, "joined or attached"; for she said "Surely this time my husband will feel affection for me, since I have given him three sons!" Her desperate longing and yearning for her husband's affection yielded no fruit. She was as unloved, and unaccepted as ever. What a personal tragedy! Finally, she learned the lesson, that her validation, acceptance, and identity come, not from her performance, or the love of any human being, but from God alone. When she had a fourth son, she named him Judah, which means, "praise"; for she said, "Now I will praise the Lord".

Only when she looked to the Lord, did she find the love and acceptance she so desperately needed. The Bible states that after Judah, she stopped having children. Her soul found its rest in God. It is little wonder that Judah became the kingly tribe in Israel, the tribe that brought forth our Lord and Savior Jesus Christ.

Leah's story is instructive for us. The Bible makes clear that our identity is not in our social media status, the number of likes or follows we have, or the love and approval of people. Our identity is not in our position, popularity, performance or possessions. Our identity is in Christ alone, and only when we look to Him for love, affirmation, value, and validation, will we be made whole. Simply stated, we are not defined by the likes of many, but by the love of one, Jesus.

We are not defined by the likes of many,
but by the love of one, Jesus.

How Aggressive Should a
Single Woman Be?

In the biblical model discussed above, the man initiates and the woman responds. The Bible has clear roles for the man and woman in a marriage, and these roles need to be established during the dating period. God's model is for the man to be the leader in the home, and the woman to respond to his lead. Since biblical dating has as its goal, the exploration of marriage for the couple, it is the perfect place to practice the biblical model of marital roles. It is important at this stage of the relationship, that the woman allow and enable the man to step into the lead role. "When men drop the ball on leadership, it presents a temptation for the woman involved to pick up the reins and lead for him. This is no less true within marriage. Picking up the reins sets a terrible pattern that only confuses the roles in the relationship and encourages both of you to take the role of the other person to the detriment of the relationship and ultimately, marriage" (*Croft*).

This means that the man should initiate the relationship by asking the woman out. I know that this involves risk, the risk of rejection. But that is an important part of being the leader. If the man doesn't esteem the woman enough to take on the risk of stepping forward to ask her out, how in the world is he going to be a husband to her and lead her through life? The willingness to risk his pride and ego, and invest in her self-esteem speaks volumes and provides the first covering for the woman. It lets her know that he cared enough for her to take a risk and has shoulders big enough to support her. The mamby-pamby men who wait around for "low hanging fruit" women to just drop from the tree all around them; men who have never believed in anything enough to be all in; men who don't know what it is to care enough to cash in their chips; men who are so insecure that they'd rather go without than bust a move; or so narcissistic that they think they are "God's gift to women"; these men who want women to pander to them, pursue them, and initiate the dating relationship, are ticking time bombs. Those character flaws will eventually show up elsewhere in the marriage when they will care more about their comfort, convenience, image, and self-esteem than the welfare of their family; when they will wait to be served, instead of serving; when they will not be willing to make any personal sacrifice for their family, and will bail out of the marriage the moment anything remotely tough appears on the horizon. These are men who will dither, wring their hands and wait around for someone to take the risk of decision making in the home, just so they can avoid blame if the decision doesn't work out. Or they will bully, argue, and use anger and verbal abuse to cover their insecurities and deficiencies. These men don't look up and dream, no that requires too much risk. They look down and pick things off the floor, things that are easy. Unfortunately, hardly anything worth having is easy, so these men live beneath their potential. If during the marriage, the woman soars, they are intimidated, become abusive, and begin to compete with and undermine her. Ladies, I think you owe it to yourself and your future to wait and give the man in your life the chance to try his hand at leadership during dating. That way if he fails, he can learn and grow before marriage, rather than jumping in there to make it "look good" and hurry him down the aisle. If you take over the reins during dating, I guarantee that you will progressively take on more and more leadership in that relationship until someday, years into your marriage, you will turn to that man with disgust and disrespect, and ask him "What is wrong with you?"

I have heard people argue that the book of Ruth provides a model for a woman to initiate a relationship with a man. In fact, I have read comments that argue that Ruth essentially proposed to Boaz. That interpretation completely omits the context. The context of the story is that Ruth acted as required under the Hebrew levirate marriage law. Ancient Israel, was a patriarchal, agrarian society where women did not inherit property. Land was divided among the tribes and passed by male inheritance. What this means is that if a woman is widowed, and has no son, her husband's inheritance will be lost. In an agrarian society where subsistence is tied to land ownership, a widowed woman can quickly become destitute if she does not have a male heir. The levirate law was intended to fill this gap. It provides that her husband's closest adult male relative should marry the widow to maintain her deceased husband's inheritance and raise up an heir. The first child born under the levirate marriage is deemed to be the heir of the deceased man, and entitled to claim his share of the inheritance.

So, Ruth was not a woman who simply met a man named Boaz, liked him, initiated with, pursued and proposed to him. No, she was acting under the express directive of her mother in law, pursuant to the rules of the levirate marriage law.

Unequally Yoked

A yoke is a wooden beam normally used between a pair of oxen or other animals in order to make them pull together on a load when working in pairs. It is a device, usually consisting of a crosspiece with two bow shaped pieces, each enclosing the head of the animal. The yoke enables the animals to walk close together when they are pulling a plow. "Equally yoked" means that oxen of comparable strength, height and capacity are teamed together, so that they can accomplish their task quickly and effectively. When two oxen are not "equally yoked", meaning that one is stronger than the other, or that one is taller than the other, the weaker or shorter ox would walk slower than the taller, stronger one, causing the load to go around in circles. "When oxen are unequally yoked, they cannot perform the task set before them. Instead of working together, they are at odds with on another" (*Unequally yoked? GotQuestions.org*).

Second Corinthians 6:14- 18 states:

> Don't team up with those who are unbelievers. How can righteousness be a partner with wickedness? How can light live with darkness? What harmony can there be between Christ and the devil? How can a believer be a partner with an unbeliever? And what union can there be between God's temple and idols? For we are the temple of the living God. As God said: "I will live in them and walk among them. I will be their God, and they will be my people. Therefore, come out from among unbelievers, and separate yourselves from them, says the LORD. Don't touch their filthy things, and I will welcome you. And I will be your Father, and you will be my sons and daughters, says the LORD Almighty.

While this scripture is not solely focused on marriage, it has the greatest and most profound application to the marriage relationship. Other partnerships have a limited impact and duration, but a spouse is a partner for life, and this partnership has tremendous, far reaching impacts that implicates future generations. Can you see the stark contrast that the scripture makes?

Believer	Unbeliever
Righteousness	Wickedness
Light	Darkness
Christ	The devil
God's temple	Idols
Filthy things	Sons & daughters of God

This scripture is clear! A believer should not team up with, partner, live or be in union with a non-believer. God's express direction is to come out from among them and separate yourself. This does not mean that you don't associate, work, or collaborate with an unbeliever. Jesus was often vilified for doing exactly that. What it does mean is that you don't get into a close bond, business partnership and certainly not marriage, with an unbeliever.

Unequally yoked can also mean that the two oxen are bearing altogether different yokes. For a yoke to work, both animals must submit to it and their heads must be encased in it. The device is intended to enable the animals to walk together side by side to accomplish their assignment. If one animal is wearing one yoke, and the other animal is wearing another, and completely different yoke, then they are not yoked together at all. They have nothing that binds them together. To an onlooker, they may appear to walk side by side, but that is until one decides to take off and go in a different direction, and there is no yoke to restrain it. Very importantly, two animals wearing two different yokes cannot pull the same plow. They will produce vastly different and discordant results.

In Matthew 11:28-30, Jesus said: "Come to me, all of you who are weary and carry heavy burdens, and I will give you rest. Take my yoke upon you. Let me teach you, because I am humble and gentle at heart, and you will find rest for your souls. For my yoke is easy to bear, and the burden I give you is light"

In this passage, Jesus informs us about His yoke and contrasts it with the yoke that is in the world. He invites the weary and heavy burdened to take His yoke which is easy and light, learn from Him and find rest. A believer takes on the yoke of Christ, and learns from Him, His worldview, ways, moral framework, and purpose. An unbeliever takes on the yoke of the devil which by implication from Jesus's description, is heavy, burdensome, hard, stressful, and leads to unrest. "For a Christian to enter into a partnership with an unbeliever is to court disaster. Unbelievers have opposite worldviews and morals, and business decisions made daily will reflect the worldview of one partner or the other. For the relationship to work, one or the other must abandon his moral center and move toward that of the other. More often than not, it is the believer who finds himself pressured to leave his Christian principles behind for the sake of profit and the growth of the business" (*Unequally Yoked, GotQuestions.org*).

If a believer wearing the yoke of Christ marries an unbeliever wearing the yoke of the devil, they will have a tortured and hazardous relationship. "No matter how respectful, sweet, or "loving" an unbelieving partner is, he is at odds with Christ – he is in rebellion." "Therefore, those of us in Christ cannot be in a harmonious, God-pleasing relationship with an unbeliever. There is no fellowship between light and darkness (2 Corinthians 7:14). The Greek word for "*fellowship*" in this passage literally means contact or intimacy. Through Paul's inspired words, we learn that intimacy with unbelievers is not just discouraged – it's *impossible*."

"No relationship apart from Christ can be truly "good" (Mark 10:18). No "love" apart from Christ is true love (1 John 4:16-17). It may look like these things from the outside, but will never be unified within" God's clear instruction to not be "unequally yoked is not meant to inhibit our dating lives. Rather it is a command designed for protection and honor. Being unequally yoked is more dangerous than you think - and waiting for someone with whom you share the same spiritual heritage is far more rewarding than many believe." (*Unequally Yoked, Masonheimer*).

Being married to an unbeliever is having the devil as your father in law!

To put it bluntly, being married to an unbeliever is having the devil as your father in law! He has the right to come into your home, marriage, health, finances, careers, and the future of your children whenever and however he wants. Are you ready for that?

My daughter just finished the eighth grade. She wanted to go to the traditional eight grade semi-formal dance. Most of her friends were going. The parents and school have been planning this event for months, and she and her friends have been talking about it non-stop for the last couple weeks – who is going, what to wear, who is going with whom, and so on. It was delightful to see them all so excited! This dance is the place to bid farewell to middle school, and go on to high school. My daughter had been asked to the dance by a young man and she turned him down. Another young man asked her rather dramatically, and literally from the roof tops – of the monkey bars at the school playground - and she also turned him down. One of her friends, a handsome and nice young man also asked to take her to the dance, as friends. She asked me about it and I said yes. He had previously been to our home for her birthday party. He is a very nice and kind young man, funny, and well behaved. I had also met his dad and believe that they are a really good family. So, I thought he was perfect. About a week to the semi-formal, he asked whether he could pick my daughter up from home for the dance. She asked me and I said yes. I was so excited! This is my daughter's first formal escort by a boy to an event. I was so proud of her! She is a beautiful young woman, inside and out, and I believe she made the right choice in the young man she picked to take her to the dance. A couple days to the dance, he touched base again to confirm that it is still okay for him to take her to the dance and we said yes! I already planned what to do with my "free time" when they went off to the dance. The day of the semi-formal arrived! In the wee hours of the morning, I got on my knees to pray for my daughter and her dance outing. As I prayed, the Lord asked me a question. He called the young man's name and asked me whether he was a Christian? I was taken aback. I did not know the answer to that question and had not thought to ask, so I told the Lord that I did not know. In the morning, I asked my daughter and she confirmed that this nice, young man had not given his heart to Jesus. The Lord's directive was clear. I could not allow my daughter to go to a middle school dance with a non-believer. This is her first formal outing with a boy, and I had to teach this truth to her. It was tough! My daughter wept, and I wept, but we had to do what we both knew was the right thing to do, to put God first in our lives. We agonized over how to cancel with the young man, at the last minute, without lying, or coming across as rude and Christian snobs. Thankfully, a real reason emerged that provided a great rationale for the cancelation. She then contacted the young man and informed him that he will not be taking her to the dance as earlier planned. After we both calmed down, I thanked the Lord that He cared enough for my daughter to make this point at this critical juncture in her life. This is a lesson that we will not soon forget – do not partner with a non-believer, no matter how nice the person is. If being unequally yoked mattered to God for an eight grade semi-formal dance, imagine how much it matters to him for marriage.

Who Shouldn't You Date?

The Girls

Ms. Waterworks: This is the girl who manipulates with her tears. She turns on the waterworks at will and they flow freely and lavishly. Whenever she does not get her way, whenever she is confronted with bad behavior, and areas of needed change, she blinks her large, doleful eyes and a river of tears gush out. Do not drown in her tears! Be firm and stand on biblical principles. Do not give in just to get her to stop crying. Think of it, if she never cried, she wouldn't have come home from the hospital when she was born. Crying never killed anybody, but compromising on the word of God will destroy your future. Don't appear heartless. Console her and calm her down. But be sure to resume the discussion at a better time. When you do, you'll likely see anger instead of tears, because she thought she got her way the first time. Ms. Waterworks is a manipulator and manipulation is witchcraft.

Ms. Nag: She is a control freak. She wears you down with her constant drip, drip, drip. She wants to control the outcomes every single time. She plays these movies in her head, and she can't stand it when the real life ending differs from the movie in her head. Solomon describes her well. Proverbs 21:9 states, "better to live on a corner on the roof than to share a home with a quarrelsome wife." And Proverbs 21:19 continues, "It's better to live alone in the desert than with a quarrelsome, complaining wife. Some women grew up in dysfunctional homes. So, for them, dysfunction is normal. If the house is too quiet, it gives them the willies; so, they stir things up, a little yelling here, a little nagging there and things are off to a rolling boil. Some wives stir up trouble just so they can have hot "make up sex!" You do not need to surrender your peace to her. Whatever you do, keep your peace! Don't let her drive you crazy. The Bible says that a quarrelsome wife is as annoying as constant dripping on a rainy day (Proverbs 27:15). You should have spotted this tendency during biblical dating. Stand up as the man, take leadership and refuse to let her destroy the peace in your home. If she is your wife, and hot sex is what she wants, schedule "hot sex" on your calendar and give it to her good, but without the emotional trauma and stress of non-stop arguments. (Keep in mind that if you are leading an ungodly lifestyle and she is pointing it out, she is not Ms. Nag.)

The Seductress: She looks succulent! Her eyes and lips drip with sensuality. She moves and swings her hips like a serpent. Her "goods" arc on display. It makes your mouth water and your throat dry just to think of it. Looking at her, well, that's just more than you can bear. It makes you weak at the knees. You feel that you did not come equipped with any mechanism to detect and avoid this creature. But that is a lie. Proverbs 5:3-22 describes her modus operandi and Proverbs 7:6-27 outlines the chilling end, utter destruction! She goes for the kill, literally! She delights in bringing down strong men, that's her specialty. Her life is a graveyard, full of great men. If you want to know the true cost of a seductress, ask Sampson about Delilah! She stripped him of his strength, his sight, his dignity, his freedom, his manhood and eventually, his life, just like the Bible warns. She is NOT worth it. Often, the seductress is not a real woman, she is a flickering image on your TV, phone or computer screen. She is a sexy, sweaty, busty daughter of Eve, looking to put her rope around your head, string you up and hang you. She is a fake woman, even her smile isn't real! She lies to you. "No one will ever know!" she says, "You can do this and get away with it". Never mind that God will know, the devil will know, and you will know. She knows that you know it is wrong, but she is a sinner and she makes sin look so hot and steamy. But the truth is, she is nothing but a snake, and the kisses and seductive noises she makes, is the hissing of the serpentine spirit in her. At last, she bites like a serpent. She sinks her fangs into you and you are hooked. She ropes and trusses you up like a turkey and you lose your freedom. Then she robs you blind! She steals your self-esteem, money, manhood, ability to be a real man with a real woman (your wife), your marriage and children. Then she heaps shame, guilt, condemnation, reproach and ridicule on you. Count the cost before you click! She is not worth it.

Ms. Shenida: Have you met Shenida? She is the desperado! Her name is pronounced She-need-a.

She-need-a man, she-need-a home, she-need-a-dollar, she-need-a-car, and so on. Shenida is the desperate woman who wants to get married by hook or by crook. She needs a man, not her man; and she will do whatever is necessary to accomplish her goal. For her, the end always justifies the means. She will dress, sex, talk, and manipulate to get what she wants. She will discount herself and compromise biblical values. She is clingy and needy. Shenida is high maintenance. She requires a lot of babysitting and hand holding. She is an amazing lure, but don't be fooled. She'll hook you and reel you in. Her ultimate trump card is pregnancy. She wants to be a baby mama, because, now's she's got you! You are trapped and she can crack the whip at will, and you'll come running. Beware of Shenida!

The Drama Queen: Ms. Drama doesn't know how to deal with life. For her, everything is a drama. She has never really grown up, and has no adult responses for life's challenges. She is a little girl in a woman's body. She routinely over-reacts and everything is a crisis. With her, life is an emotional roller coaster. She goes from one extreme to another. She loves attention, rolls her eyes, is loud and abrasive. She is no lady! She makes mountains out of mole hills, and wears her heart and emotions on her sleeve. There is no peace with the drama queen. Its always something. She talks about how interesting her life is, but it's all drama, and she doesn't know the difference. She has no discretion. She is not self-aware. She is loud and crass. She can look all dolled up and sweet one minute, and the next be cursing someone out and reeling for a fist fight. Don't hook up with her! Your life will become one bad movie. Whenever you want some drama, you can pay $10 and visit her in the movie theater, but you don't have to bring her home with you. She is good only on the movie screen, she's not good to live with.

Bargain Basement Woman: This is the woman who does not value herself. She has low self-esteem and precious little self-worth. To use a car analogy, she is like a Geo Metro. Her personal vibe shouts "no credit, bad credit, no job, everybody welcome". She thinks she is "damaged goods" and so, latches on to whatever and whoever comes down the pike. Her older sister is Shenida, she is best friends with Ms. Waterworks, and her twin sister is woe-is-me. She doesn't value or love herself and so cannot genuinely love or value anybody else. She is perennially insecure and you have to constantly fill her up with words of affirmation to keep her afloat. If you miss a day, she is deflated and flat. At first you like her because she doesn't have an opinion. She is like the arranged wife in the Eddie Murphy movie, "Coming to America". Her constant response is, "whatever you want honey". You liked it at first, because you felt like "the man". Then you realize that there is a problem. The lights are on, but nobody is home. Now her insecurity drives you crazy because she perpetually checks up on you, thinks you are cheating on her or about to leave her. You know she needs help and wonder how she can be the mother of your children. How will your kids turn out under her daily influence? The answer is simple, don't date or marry her!

Gold Digger: Ms. Gold likes the finer things in life, and she believes she deserves them and should be able to have them. So, she sets about to do just that. She is the woman who thinks that life and love is a transaction. I give you my "love" and you give me money. She is a kept woman, a trophy wife, or wants to be. Don't misunderstand, she is not a street walker. She loves fast cars, fancy clothes, fine dining, and picket fenced houses. She absolutely enjoys shopping; for her, it is retail therapy. She doesn't like to work, but she is a slave driver! She drives her man to work to pay for all her wants. Her credit card bills are mortgage sized. She needs so much to make her feel wanted and valued. There is a gaping void in her, and she is desperately stuffing money, clothes, cars, vacations, everything down into this hole, but it never fills up. She's pretty as a picture, but has no skills, except bedroom skills. The worst thing is, she doesn't know who she is. Her

identity is in her status and the things she accu-
mulates, so when they are not there, she is lost. So,
she has to keep the cash flowing, as soon as the
cash trails off, so does her love. If her man flags or
flails in body or finances, she can't handle it. She
doesn't miss a beat. She is off with another man in
a flash. She is not a long term "for better or worse"
kind of girl. If you are looking for a soul mate, she
is not your girl. Her soul mate is Mr. Money.

The Guys

The Player: Mr. Player fancies himself as a sensual,
smooth, ladies' man, but the long and short of it is
that he is a sex addict. He is ready to solicit a prostitute, hookup with an old date, or do anything for
sex. This is the guy who treats women like bread.
Bread comes in different shapes, sizes, flavors and
grains. He likes to taste them all. For him, "dating"
is a code word for sex on demand. He will take whatever he can get. Anything in skirts works. He is the
guy who is calling and trying to make up with you
after a break-up, and in the interim, will sleep with
another woman while waiting to hear back from
you. Beware of the player! He talks a good game,
but is not planning to stick around for the long haul.
He doesn't want a real woman and can't handle a
real woman. Why? Because he is not a real man! A
real man is a man who can satisfy one woman for

a lifetime. Jumping from one woman to another, that's child's play, boys do that. The player is the guy who buys you dinner, and thinks that would get him into your bed. Often players are powerful men or men in positions of authority. They are used to getting what they want. They do not take no for an answer. If he can't get sex for free when he wants it, he'll pay for it. Mr. Player is charming, intelligent and educated. But his brain is between his legs. He carries on with multiple women at the same time. He says that he wants genuine love and marriage. But his sexual appetite has been stretched far beyond what God intended, such that no normal woman can satisfy him. He has a spirit of lust and has devolved into sexual addiction. The bible says to stay away from this guy (2 Corinthians 5:11).

The Grinch: This guy is harsh in word and deed. He thinks that being a man is being hard, brusque, abusive, and abrasive. He thinks he is a strong man, who does not let women control him, but the truth is that he is a weak man, who mistakes stubbornness and lack of empathy for strength. Mr. Grinch had been hurt in the past and now has his guard up. He wants to hurt you first before you can hurt him. He is mean spirited and bitter, and the vitriol spills out through his mouth. Mr. Grinch has a bad temper, and whenever he chats with you, he dumps his junk on you. He is a talker too! He is always complaining about something or someone. Somebody always does him wrong, and the way he tells it, he is always the responsible one, and an all-around great guy. Mr. Grinch is "trashman". He deals in trash and treats people like trash, because that's all he knows. He prides himself on his stability, responsibility, and steady income. But his heart is unhappy, and he is infectious. The Bible says to stay away from him! Proverbs 22:24 says, Don't befriend angry people or associate with hot-tempered people, or you will learn to be like them and endanger your soul".

The Narcissist: Mr. Narcissist is the guy who believes that he is God's gift to womankind. He is in love with himself and absolutely convinced that he is irresistible. He loves to hear his own voice, and every conversation is a song that he sings to himself. It goes like this, "how great thou art". He thinks that he is the center of the universe, and women exist to cater to his every need and desire. He is extremely insecure, with a fragile ego, and becomes very irate and abusive if his version of reality is threatened. He belittles the women in his life, and verbally abuses them, because that makes him feel good about himself. He has to claw, bite, and climb on the back of others to rise. He is egotistical, and likes to work out, so he can show off his good looks. Mr. Narcissist looks good enough to eat, but he is tough to swallow. He leaves a sour taste in your mouth every time you meet him. He likes women to pander to him and pursue him. He is a good dresser, because he wants to impress the girls. He wants them to swoon when he makes his appearance. Sometimes, Mr. Narcissist starts out being the "provider", but not for long. He likes to be "kept" by his women - fancy clothes, high end accessories, and endless pairs of expensive shoes. His "work" consists of bilking women out of their money, and if you say NO, he hints, ever so subtly, that he may be leaving you, and moving in with Suzie, who is happy to treat him the way he deserves. Well, give him what he deserves, the boot!

The Controller: This is the emperor. The self-appointed Czar! He wants to control and rule his women with an iron fist. This is his definition of "manhood". He controls his babes with anger, fear, and sometimes money. He calls you at all times of the day and night because he is "thinking about you", but the real reason is, he wants to check up on you. He is very insecure and is deeply afraid. He knows who he really is, deep inside, and is deathly afraid that you will wise up and leave him. He doesn't like it when you want to do your own thing, or hang out with your family and friends. He wants to be the center of your universe, and cut you off from everybody else. He tells you stories of how his former women where submissive beauties. Like the devil, he quotes the bible too. His favorite scripture is Ephesians 5:22, "Wives, submit to your husbands as to the Lord". He completely skips over the part that says, "Men love your wives as Christ loves the church and gave Himself for her". The controller is not giving himself for anyone. He is a self-centered, self-absorbed, my-way-or-the-highway, kind of guy. His motto is, me, myself, and I. You should not date the controller, and if you are already dating him, leave as soon as you can, but be careful, because when you tell him that you want to break up with him, he will go insane! So, do it from a safe distance, or in a public place, and refuse to meet with him privately. Mr. controller can't stand to be ignored, much less disrespected or dumped! But that is exactly where he belongs, in the dumps.

The Married Hunter: Mr. Hunt is the nice, gentle, soft spoken guy who is not satisfied with one woman. But he doesn't say that! He is a smooth operator. He tells you a sob story about how his marriage is unhappy and his wife is not meeting his needs. He doesn't mention his philandering, or the children he will abandon. He changes women like jobs, and with jobs. When things get tough, instead of standing up and working through them like a man, he scrams and looks for the next woman. It's all about him, his desires, feelings, and needs. He deserves to be happy, never mind what his action will do to others. Be on the alert, Mr. Hunt comes in two models, first model Mr. Hunt wants you as his mistress, a side dish of hot sex on the side. He tells you he will leave his wife, but never will. Most women are familiar with first model Mr. Hunt, but the other model is not well known. Second model Mr. Hunt is not afraid of commitment, in fact, that is his tool. He dangles commitment. It is his lure. He will divorce his wife and marry you if you will say yes, but for how long? Mr. Hunt loves toys, adult toys, like big houses, and big cars, fully loaded. Mr. Hunt will wine and dine you until you say yes! He would sweep you off your feet. He is nice, compassionate and supportive. He is every woman's dream. Unfortunately, this is the man who has never grown up, does not know how to handle life and lives on luxury lane. He lives only for himself. True to his name, Mr. Hunt sizes up and picks out his quarry. The workplace is his hunting ground. He has "elevator eyes". He is a looker too, and seems like the nicest, and most supportive guy ever. But he will say whatever he needs to say to get you to say yes. Beware of Mr. Hunt, the dis-arming, stable, demure guy, that is anything but. He has blood on his hands, the blood of distraught women, and abandoned kids. If you say yes to him, you will be wife number three, or four or five. But soon, when you are not new and shiny anymore, or you refuse to jump when he says so, he will leave you for the next woman. My question is, what are you doing with Mr. Hunt? He is a married man! Married men are off limits (Mark 10:9). So, get yourself up and out!

The User: Mr. Shrew is a user. He uses everyone in his path. For him, people are a means to an end. He is shrewd and calculating. He doesn't give something for nothing. He is the barter king, he buys and trades people all the time. He knows how to talk the talk, different strokes for different folks. He is a good story teller, his jokes will make you laugh, but all the while, he is manipulating you, checking out your boundaries, parameters and vulnerabilities. He will take everything he can, and leave in the morning with no twinge of conscience. He is ruthless and heartless. It's all about profit, his profit. This is why Mr. User will not contemplate marriage. No woman will put a brand on him! His bachelor status is his lure. He enjoys flirting with women and making them dream of being married to him. But unlike the hotshot image he portrays, he is a hollow man, a straw man, a man with no heart. He cheats without batting an eyelid. He will wine and dine you on somebody else's dime. Mr. User is a nightmare, a disaster waiting to happen. Give him a wide berth!

Mr. Alimony: Mr. Gold is the alimony guy! He looks real humble and would do and say anything to make you feel happy and valued. But he is not for real. He is working for hire. He likes your lifestyle, that's all. He plans to have you bankroll his laziness. He wants the status symbol of being with you. You are an elegant, sophisticated, classy, accomplished woman. He wants you on his arm, so he can show you off. He wants you to elevate his stature. He looks deep into your eyes and in a deep voice says, "baby, I can't stop thinking about you". But that is a lie. He's just thinking about your money. He has a grand vision of himself living the high life with your alimony. He wants to marry you today. He is ready, because as soon as you say "I do", then he does! Laughing all the way to the bank. He can't wait to get his hands on your money. Second. Thessalonians 3:6,10 warns you of this guy. Stay away from lazy-bones and don't feed him neither! It's simple, "Those unwilling to work will not get to eat".

CHAPTER 6

EMPOWERED

THE NEXT PREEMINENT STEP TO WHOLENESS
is power, God's power. The E in WHOLE is for
"Empowered". Empowered means to give someone the
authority, right or power to be or do something. It means
to authorize, license, commission, delegate, qualify,
and enable someone. It also means to make someone
stronger, and more confident; and in this sense, empowerment sets people free, and enables them to be and
accomplish all that they were created for.

"Empowered" could mean almost anything in today's
world, but for the Christian single, it means only one
thing, being filled with, and led by the Holy Spirit. Acts
1:8 states, "You will receive power when the Holy Spirit
comes upon you." John 1:12 confirms, "But to all who
believed Him and accepted Him, He gave the power
to become children of God". And Romans 8:14 con-
cludes, "For all who are led by the Spirit of God are
children of God".

*For all who are led by the spirit of God are
the children of God.*

Who Is the Holy Spirit?

He is the third person in the Godhead. He is one with the Father and the Son (1 John 5:7). He is the Spirit of God, the Spirit of Christ, and the dunamis power of God. He is the energy force of the Godhead, the divine midwife who gives birth to the plans and purposes of God. He is the creative energy of God who hovered over the dark and empty earth in Genesis 1:2, to bring forth creation. The Holy Spirit is a person, with a mind, will, and emotions. He loves, (Romans 15:30, Romans 5:5, Galatians 5:22); has a will (1 Corinthians 12:11); has a mind, (Romans 8:27); and has thought, knowledge, and understanding (1 Cor 2:10-13). The Holy Spirit has emotions, such as grief and sorrow (Ephesians 4:30); insult and out- rage, (Hebrews 10:29); and can be lied to and tempted (Acts 5: 3-4).

The Holy Spirit is the heavenly power source resident on the earth today. It is He who energizes the will of God, giving it life and substance. When the Bible says in Philippians 2:13, that "God is working in you, giving you the desire and the power to do what pleases him", it is talking about the Holy Spirit. He is the One who breathes God's life into any situation. The Hebrew word for the Holy Spirit is Ruach; and the Greek word is Pneuma. Both words mean "wind or breath". In Ezekiel 37, where the prophet saw a vision of the valley full of dry bones, even after the bones had joined together, and were covered with flesh, and had become a great army, they lay lifeless, until the prophet, at the direction of God, called forth the "Breath" of God (Ezekiel 37:9-10). The same thing happened in Genesis 2:7. After God formed man from the dust of the earth, he was lifeless until God breathe into him "the breath of life". Only then did man become a living person. The Holy Spirit is the Breath of God. He brings the life of God into any situation or circumstance.

It is the work of the Holy Spirit to bring forth and give birth to the life and will of God. His role in our lives is to empower us to become like Christ, and live a victorious Christian life. This is why Jesus told His disciples to wait for the Holy Spirit (Luke 24:49). You cannot do anything of eternal consequence without the Holy Spirit. Indeed, you cannot live a successful Christian life without Him. And when He came in Acts 2:2, He came as "a rushing mighty wind".

The Role of the Holy Spirit

In John 14:26 Jesus said, "But the Helper, the Holy Spirit, whom the Father will send in My name, He will teach you all things, and bring to your remembrance all that I said to you." The Amplified version uses seven words to outline the role or job description of the Holy Spirit. He is the Comforter, Counselor, Helper, Intercessor, Advocate, Strengthener, and Standby. Since the work of the Holy Spirit is to help us to become more like Christ, His job description gives you an insight into what it is we are empowered to do.

The Holy Spirit represents Christ, and acts on His behalf. He seals or marks the believer with the favor, protection, ownership and authority of God, (Ephesians 1:13 -14, John 1:33, Acts 10:47-48), teaches believers, (John 14: 26), gives us power to be a witness for Christ (Acts 1:8), maintains fellowship with us, and facilitates our fellowship with the Father, (2 Cor 13:14); lives in our bodies as his temple, (1 Cor 6:19); helps us in our weaknesses - areas where we are prone to sin, failure, deficiency or inadequacy, (Romans 8:26); equips us for service, (Acts 6:3), guides us into all truth, (John 16:13); helps us administer the resources, plans, and agenda of God, (1 Corinthians 12:11); sanctifies us (Romans 15:16), leads us (Luke 4:1), spreads the love of God in our hearts (Romans 5:5), and so much more. Simply stated, we desperately need and cannot suc- ceed without the ministry of the Holy Spirit!

Empowered To Be

The Holy Spirit empowers us to be. We live in a time and culture where there is an inordinate emphasis on doing. We are constantly inundated with activity, noise, and over-stimulation. If you announce to your friends and coworkers that you are going on vacation, you are immediately bombarded with questions about what you are going to do? You can never just "be" on vacation. To many people, to just "be", is synonymous with boring and lonely. But that is not the truth of the scriptures. God is very invested in our being. He places our WHO above, and before our DO. He is completely committed to us being and becoming. That is the sum total of the empowering work of the Holy Spirit in our lives - to help us to be and to become. WHOLE singles are men and women who are becoming through the power of the indwelling Holy Spirit.

Becoming Who We Are

In Genesis 1:26-27, God said:

> Let us make man in our image, according
> to our likeness and let them have dominion
> over the fish of the sea, and the birds of the
> air and over the cattle and over all of the
> earth and every creeping thing that creeps
> on the earth. God created man in his own
> image, in the image of God he created him.
> Male and female he created them.

"In Genesis 1, we see a pattern. When God wanted to create anything, he spoke to the source of the thing. In verse 11 God said: "Let the land sprout with vegetation. . .. And it was so." In verse 20 God said, "Let the waters swarm with fish and other life . . . and . . . Let the skies be filled with birds of every kind. . .. And it was so." In verse 24, God said, "Let the earth bring forth every sort of animal. . .. And it was so." The pattern is, God speaks to the source of the thing to be created to bring forth and it brought forth. When it came time to make man, God spoke to Himself. He said, "Let us make man in our image, according to our likeness." God is our source of origin, not tadpoles, a big bang, or anything else. Mankind came from God. We are His offspring (Acts 17:28).

Whole singles are men and women who are "becoming" through the power of the indwelling Holy Spirit.

God reproduced us after His kind—the god kind. He made us only just a little lower than Himself and delegated to us authority over all of creation (Psalm 8). "We are like God, having His attributes, nature and capable of manifesting His power. First John 4:17(b) KJV states that as He, Jesus, is, so are we in this world. We are made in the image and likeness of Almighty God. An image is an authentic representation of a person or thing and likeness is the capacity to resemble, replicate, or reproduce that person or thing. We are an authentic representation of God in the earth and have the capacity to reproduce Him, His love, character, grace, and so forth on the earth" *(Godson)*. The work of the Holy Spirit is to help us to become who we are, sons and daughters of God.

Romans 8:29 states, "For God knew His people in advance, and He chose them to become like His Son, so that His Son would be the firstborn among many brothers and sisters". Jesus is the pattern son, and the work of the Holy Spirit in our lives is to help us to become like Christ, and operate as "sons" of God in the earth. "God our Father wants us to walk in the rights, authority and privileges of sonship. This was His express intent, plan, and purpose. He wanted us to occupy and rule over the earth, acting in His stead, as God. The mission of the Holy Spirit in our lives is to help us to understand the full meaning and implications of sonship, establish our destiny and birthright as "sons" of God, and empower us to walk in the privileges and rights of sonship. The ultimate goal of God is to enable us to follow and reproduce the pattern—Jesus is the pattern Son. God wants every Christian to grow and mature from children into sonship until we look like Jesus in word and deed.

Note that new covenant sonship is not about gender (Romans 8:14). Rather, it is, "knowing my identity in Christ and walking in it! It means recognizing the nature, attributes, and capabilities of God within me until it moves me to act like God on the earth. As a "son" of God, I am the spitting image of Christ: I look exactly like Jesus in my spirit. I simply need to believe it and allow what is already in my spirit to manifest through my soul and rule over my body" (*Godson*).

A whole single in on a lifelong quest to become like Christ. We are "under construction", and the foreman is the Holy Spirit. This construction project will go on throughout our lifetime. Ruth Graham, the wife of world renowned evangelist Billy Graham died in 2007. The epitaph on her tombstone came from a road sign she once saw. It simply states, "end of construction – thank you for your patience". One day like Ruth, the end of construction will come for us when we see Jesus face to face, and know Him, even as we are known.

Empowered to Do

God has given us His Holy Spirit to empower us to do. Ephesians 2:10 states that, "We are God's masterpiece. He has created us anew in Christ Jesus, so we can do the things He planned for us long ago." As we submit to the "becoming" work of the Holy Spirit, we naturally begin to do. Becoming is an internal process, it is a heart affair. Becoming is critical because God focuses on the heart. He said in 1 Samuel 16:7, "Man looks on the outward appearance, but the Lord looks at the heart". Becoming is the goal, but the key evidence, manifestation, or outworking of the becoming process, is the doing. Daniel 11:32b encapsulates this truth. It states, "The people who know their God, shall be strong and do exploits." Note that the people who know their God shall first "be" and then "do". This is because if your doing doesn't come from a deeper place of being, it will never accomplish the purposes of God. This is the work of the Holy Spirit, to help us to be and then to do.

God has things that "He planned for us" to do. Jeremiah 29:11 elaborates, "I know the plans I have for you says the Lord. They are plans for good and not for disaster, to give you a future and a hope". As we "become", we are able to discern, recognize, and do His good plans (Romans 12:1-2). Philippians 2:13 sums it up, "For it is God who works in you both to will and to do of His good pleasure." The "God who works in you", is the Holy Spirit.

The outward evidence of the inward working of God is that we begin to bear fruit. This is the purest evidence of the life of God in us, when we begin to naturally bear the fruit of God. You see, an orange tree may look like any other tree, but during fruit season, it will bring forth oranges, the distinctive fruit that marks, and sets it apart as an orange tree. In John 15:5, Jesus said, "I am the vine; you are the branches. Those who remain in me, and I in them, will produce much fruit. For apart from me you can do nothing". This is the litmus test, fruit! If we are truly "becoming", then there will be the evidence of good fruit in our lives.

This means that you cannot authentically be a child of God without producing fruit that reflects the nature of God, and you cannot produce the god-kind fruit without the help, transformation, tutoring, agency, and partnership of the Holy Spirit. "That is why Jesus instructed the apostles to do nothing until they received the Holy Spirit. "Wait for Him", Jesus said, because any work done without partnership with the Holy Spirit breaks the sonship mold. It is "strange fire"; fruitless work that will be burned up" (Godson).

Galatians 5:22-23 describes the fruit that will showcase the life of God in us and the work of the Holy Spirit. It states, "But the Holy Spirit produces this kind of fruit in our lives: love, joy, peace, patience, kindness, goodness, faithfulness, gentleness, and self-control. There is no law against these things!" Note that this list of god-kind attributes is collectively called "fruit" and not "fruits". It is one fruit, a full complement or portfolio of fruit produced by the Holy Spirit, and it comes as a package. This means that when we become children of God, we have the capacity to produce this entire package of fruit. We must not let the devil deceive us into an a la carte mindset, where we pick and choose which Christ-like attributes to produce, or think that we are impotent to produce one or the other. I have heard Christians say how they can be loving, kind, and gentle, but cannot control themselves around a particular type of dessert, or do not have patience. While that may be the fact, it is not the truth. The entire fruit package is deposited in us by the Holy Spirit, but like all other things in the word of God, it is in seed form. We need to cultivate the seed of self-control and patience to produce the fruit of self-control and patience in our lives. It is like a muscle that we develop through training and constant use (Hebrews 5:14).

The Holy Spirit also empowers us to do, through the distribution of His gifts. First Corinthians 12:4-10 lists nine gifts of the Holy Spirit. They are, word of wisdom, word of knowledge, faith, healings, miracles, prophecy, discerning of spirits, ability to speak in unknown languages, and the ability to interpret what is being said. Romans 12:6-8, lists other ministry gifts such as, prophecy, service, teaching, encouraging, giving, leadership ability, and showing kindness. And Ephesians 4:11-12, lists the five-fold ministry gifts of apostles, prophets, teachers, evangelists, and pastors, that Christ gave to build up the church.

The Bible is clear, everyone has a gift. The Holy Spirit makes sure of that. He alone decides which gift each person should have (1 Corinthians 12:11), and distributes them accordingly. Now, we must be careful. While the gifts are given by the Holy Spirit, they can sometimes be deployed and exercised without the power of the Holy Spirit. They can, for example, be powered by charisma, momentum, sheer force of personality, natural talent, human applause, manipulation, and so on. Also, they can be counterfeited by the devil and operate through demonic power (Acts 16:16-18). This is why, unlike fruit, gifts are not the tell-tale evidence of the life of God in a person.

What is the Difference Between Gifts and Fruit?

1. Gifts can be counterfeited, but fruit cannot.

2. Gifts are outward demonstrations, but fruit is the evidence and outgrowth of inward transformation.

3. Gifts are manifested in, and are limited to this earth, but fruit is the nature of God, and endures eternally.

4. God's gifts and calling are irrevocable (Romans 11:29), so someone can walk away from God, and still "manifest" the gifts of the Holy Spirit, but that is not the case with the fruit of the Holy Spirit. If you walk away from Him, you will wither, and will not bring forth any fruit (John 15:6).

5. You can display and manifest the gifts and go to hell (Matthew 7:21-23, but you cannot bring forth the fruit of the Holy Spirit and go to hell. This is because the word of God has enough power in itself to bring itself to pass. And, the name of Jesus is above every name, and at His name, every knee shall bow (Philippians 2:10). So, the fact that the word of God and the name of Jesus are used to manifest the gifts, and performs miracles, is not an endorsement of the person using the Word or the name.

6. Gift is what we do, while fruit is how and why we do it. Fruit displays our nature, the nature of God within us.

Empowered to Love

For the Christian single, or single again, the Holy Spirit can empower you to love or love again. He specializes in healing broken hearts and lives. He can restore the broken places in your life, and empower you to dream again. With the Holy Spirit as your guide, you can find love again. He can empower you to believe again, trust again, be vulnerable again, and be married again!

Empowered to Live Single

Let's face it, life is altogether challenging, and the single lifestyle is no less so. Singleness has its unique challenges and stresses. Many singles complain of loneliness, depression, isolation, uncertainty about the future, fear of never finding the right person, lack of financial independence, and so on. The Holy Spirit is the only person who can help you navigate these issues successfully.

Many singles are single parents. They daily confront the challenge of raising children alone, playing the dual role of father and mother, while working to provide financially for their children. One major issue faced by singles is making decisions alone. Many singles lack support and have to struggle alone to evaluate all the options, and come to the right choices in decision making. This is particularly challenging for single parents who have to make weighty decisions for the future of their children all by themselves.

Other singles are forced to contend with their Ex's current spouse, or crazy girl, or boy friend. These entanglements complicate issues and, if not handled right, can have the potential to foment significant stress in the life of a Christian single.

For single women, there is the challenge of routine life, car, house, and home maintenance requirements that are traditionally male roles, but the single woman finds herself thrust into these roles. Many single women have to learn to change tires, smoke detectors, and pump gas. Same thing with single men, who have to learn how to cook, clean, keep house, do laundry, and other traditionally female roles.

Some singles have grown children, and are dealing with the challenges associated with being an empty nester, and transitioning their role from being needed as a mom or dad, to being a mentor, sounding board, and cheer leader; allowing their child to make their own decisions. These singles struggle with questions and issues of personal significance, insecurity, and role relevance.

The Holy Spirit equips, empowers, and enables every Christian single to overcome these challenges. The work of the Holy Spirit is to build character, integrity, consistency, confidence, and security in the individual, as well as faith, and reliance on the finished works of Jesus Christ. These godly convictions are based on principles which are backed by the person, character, and power of God.

Holy Spirit Baptism

Have you received the Holy Spirit? It is impossible to live a victorious Christian life without Him. Here is God's promise:

> "'In the last days,' God says, 'I will pour out my Spirit upon all people. Your sons and daughters will prophesy. Your young men will see visions, and your old men will dream dreams. In those days I will pour out my Spirit even on my servants—men and women alike— and they will prophesy" (Acts 2:17-18).

Ask God to baptize you with His Holy Spirit. This is when the Holy Spirit fills you up inside and you begin to speak in a different tongue/language when you pray (Acts 2). To receive the Holy Spirit, pray this prayer:

Lord Jesus, you are the one who baptizes with the Holy Spirit. John the Baptist said, "I baptize you with water for repentance. But after me comes one who is more powerful than I, whose sandals I am not worthy to carry. He will baptize you with the Holy Spirit and fire" (Matthew 3:11). I ask you now to baptize me with your Holy Spirit - Amen!

Note that you receive the person of the Holy Spirit the same way you received the gift of salvation - by faith. There are no fireworks or magic feelings. Simply believe that you received the Holy Spirit when you asked in prayer, then open your mouth and speak - not your native or learned language, but in the new language given to you by God. Keep in mind that you will not understand what you are saying. So, the devil will tell you that you are making it up, that you are speaking gibberish, that it is fake, and that nothing happened. He is a liar and a thief. He wants to steal God's precious gift from you. Don't let him! You may feel silly speaking a language you don't understand, but don't let that stop you. Just like any other language, your proficiency in your new prayer language will grow with practice. So, continue to speak in your new language every time you pray and see the power of God released in your life!

AFTERWORD

GOD WANTS EVERY CHRISTIAN SINGLE TO be whole. He wants us to live lives filled with His presence, purpose, passion, and power. But so many singles live with a fragmented soul; areas of the soul that have been vandalized by the devil through toxic relationships, circumstances, wrong thinking, and different types of bondage. God wants to heal and restore these broken areas of our lives. He wants to take our ashes and give us His beauty.

This book outlines five practical steps to wholeness in the spirit, soul, and body. Simply stated, there is no wholeness without wellness, health, passion for God, a loving heart, and the power of the Holy Spirit. These are five truths that frame the portrait of an abundant life, a life that is free from bondage and oppression. This book includes prayer outlines to break free from the bondage of curses and satanic covenants, soul ties and spiritual orbits, as well as deliverance from demonic oppression and personal vows. God wants you to be whole and free. This book shows you how.

My prayer is that you will read this book and apply its truths to every area of your life. I proclaim that this book will help you, and millions of God's people to be made whole, and to walk in the glorious liberty of the sons and daughters of God! If you have not received Jesus as your Lord and savior, I urge and encourage you to pray the following prayer:

"Lord Jesus, I confess that I have sinned against you. Thank you for dying on the cross for me. I believe in you. Please forgive my sins, come into my heart and be my Lord and savior. Fill me with your Holy Spirit. Thank you for giving me power, and victory over sin, my flesh, the devil, and the world. Help me to live a life that honors you daily – Amen!"

ACKNOWLEDGMENTS

1. Every book is the result of the work of a team, and this book is no exception.

2. Thank you to my friend and partner the Holy Spirit, at whose persistent nudging I finally wrote this book.

3. Thanks to my children, Emmanuel, Timothy and Rhema, whose support, encouragement and love kept me motivated.

4. Thanks to the *Saved Singles Summit* Team, whose partnership and hard work made the Saved Singles Summit events so successful.

5. Thanks to my friends who provided their thoughts and feedback on this book.

6. Thanks to my project team at Xulon Press, Sylvia Burleigh, Alexandria Zaldivar, and the whole team. Working with you was a joy.

7. I am deeply grateful to God my Father, and the Lord Jesus Christ, for Your grace and power that has kept me sexually pure and free in spirit, soul, and body.

8. This book is a joint effort by many. I am truly grateful for the opportunity to partner with you all. I am better because of you.

NOTES

CHAPTER 1: WHOLENESS
1.   Merriam Webster's Dictionary
2.   Choosing A Life of Victory, Gloria Godson, Xulon Press, 2019.
3.   On Death and Dying, Elizabeth Kubler Ross
4.   Dr. David Hoffeditz, "They Were Single Too: Eight Biblical Role Models", (ThM, 1996.

CHAPTER 2: WELL
1.   Nothing, Mick Inkpen, Hodder Children's Books
2.   Let's Stop Comparing Ourselves: 6 Ways Jealousy is Stealing Your Self Love & How to Stop It, Aabye-Gayle, August 30, 2018.
3.   Comparison is not the Thief of Joy, Abigail Dodds, March 26, 2018.
4.   10 Health Problems Related to Stress That You Can Fix, R Morgan Griffin, WebMD.
5.   The Biblical Illustrator, Electronic Database, D Roberts, D. D., 2011.

CHAPTER 3: HEALTH
1.   The World Health Organization's Definition of Health: Social Versus Spiritual Health, James S Larson, March 15, 1996.

2. The Spiritual Dimension: its importance to patients' health, well-being and quality of life and its implications for nursing practice, Ross L. International Journal of Nursing Studies, Volume 32, Issue 5, October 1995.

3. What is Spiritual Health? – Definition & Examples, Online Course, Study.com.

4. Healing the Soul of a Woman, Joyce Meyer, Faith Words, 2018.

5. Mental health: a state of well-being, World Health Organization, August 2014.

6. Why is Mental Health So Difficult to Define? Christopher Lane Ph.D., June 2016.

7. Mental Health: Keeping Your Emotional Health, Article, familydoctor.org.

8. 7 Signs of Emotional Wellness, Dr. Shannon Kolakowski, October 2013.

9. The Searing of the Christian Conscience, Steve Gallagher, January 2016.

10. Amazing Facts About the Human Eye, Key -Whitman Eye Center, Blog, July.

11. The Holiness of God, John McArthur, Grace to You, Code GTY100.

12. Holiness of God – God's Attributes, All About God.com.

13. Top 5 Health-Related Components of Fitness, Tyler Read, November 23, 2017.

14. (Stillness and Rest: An Essential Part of Health, Dr. Deborah Anderson, Huffpost, January 28, 2016)

15. How to Keep a Positive Attitude When You Don't Feel Like It, Blog, Dr. Alan Zimmerman, July 11, 2017.

16. The Value of Human Suffering by Wayne Jackson, ChristianCourier.Com.

CHAPTER 4: ON-FIRE

1. The Zeal Of The Lord, A Sermon Published on November 12, 1914, Delivered by C. H. Spurgeon.

2. What is a Eunuch in the Bible, Got Questions, Your Questions, Biblical Answers, gotquestions.org.

3. Choosing a Life of Victory, Gloria Godson, Xulon Press 2019.

4. 10 Rules to Live by for Singles, Blog, Gloria Godson, SavedSinglesSummit.com

CHAPTER 5: LOVING

1. Zavada, Jack. "4 Types of Love in the Bible." Learn Religions, Apr. 17, 2019, learnreligions. com/types-of-love-in-the-bible-700177.

2. Are You A Narcissist? The Common Signs & Symptoms of Narcissistic Personality Disorder, Katherine George, June 7th, 2018.

3. Spirit Controlled Temperament, Dr. Tim LaHaye, Tyndale House Publishers 1993.

4. Know Yourself? 6 Specific Ways to Know Who You Are, Meg Selig Changepower, Article, Psychology Today, March 9, 2016.

5. The Samaritan Schism, Schisms in Jewish History: Part 2, Lawrence H Schiffman, Article, Bible History Daily, August 11, 2014.

6. Fatal Attractions, Jack Hayford, Regal Books, 2004.

7. 6 Ways to "Be Holy for I am Holy", Aretha Grant, Article, 1Believe.com

8. What Does The Bible Actually Say About Dating? Debra Fileta, February 15, 2016.

9. Biblical Dating: How it's Different From Modern Dating, by Scott Croft, March 23, 2007.

10. Biblical Dating: Men Initiate, women Respond, Focus on the Family, Scott Croft, February 15, 2007.

11. What Does it mean to be unequally yoked? GotQuestions.org.

12. Why Being Unequally Yoked Is More Dangerous Than You Think, Phylicia Masonheimer, Crosswalk.com Blog, February 22, 2017.

CHAPTER 5: EMPOWERED

1. Choosing A Life Of Victory, Gloria Godson, Xulon Press, 2019.

OTHER BOOKS BY
THE AUTHOR

Choosing a Life of Victory, Gloria Godson, Xulon Press 2019.

ADDITIONAL TEACHINGS/ RESOURCES BY THE AUTHOR

1. Choosing a Life of Victory,
2. The Finished Works of Christ
3. What is in Your Mouth?
4. The Unstoppable God
5. The Holy Spirit, my Friend & Partner
6. What Will You Sow in Your Life in 2018?
7. A Woman of Character
8. Character Counts
9. Kingdom Prayer
10. Jesus is Praying for You
11. Praying the Names of God
12. Praying Through Ephesians
13. Alpha & Omega, The God of Time
14. The Ministry of Intercession
15. The Power of Prayer and Fasting
16. Sons of God, Who are They?
17. Does Jesus Value Women?
18. What is Your Nickname?
19. Altars and Priesthoods
20. Prayers in the Bible
21. The Release of His Power
22. Solitude – Alone with God
23. Curses, Covenants and How to Break Them

THE SAVED SINGLES SUMMIT

The Author hosts *The Saved Singles Summit*, a premier Christ-centered forum, which brings together Christian singles from area churches for a day of fun, empowerment, fellowship, kingdom connections and new opportunities.

Join us:
www.savedsinglessummit.com
Facebook@savedsinglessummit
Instagram@savedsinglesummit

THE GRACETALK

The Author hosts *The GraceTalk*, a weekly show/podcast.

Join us: www.thegracetalk.com
Facebook@thegracetalk

YouTube: The GraceTalk

CPSIA information can be obtained
at www.ICGtesting.com
Printed in the USA
BVHW081451090321
602112BV00004B/168